D1433347

BY YON BONNIE LINKS!

St Andrews Old Course Hotel – 1990 version – dominates the Road Hole. (Inset) Its predecessor – once likened to 'an old oak chest with the drawers pulled out'. *(See pages 113–115)*

BY YON BONNIE LINKS!

A 'Mixed Bag' of
14 Auld Clubs!

Sam Morley

Aedificamus Press

First Published 1990
Aedificamus Press, The Ridgeway,
Northaw, Herts, EN6 4BG

ISBN 0 9511701 4 7

Typeset by Ryburn Typesetting Ltd, Luddendenfoot, Halifax

Printed in Great Britain by
The Amadeus Press Ltd, Huddersfield

British Library Cataloguing in Publication Data

Morley, Sam
By Yon Bonnie Links!: A 'Mixed Bag' of 14 Auld Clubs!
    1. Scotland, Golf Courses
    I. Title
    796. 352. 068411

ISBN 0-9511701-4-7

Contents

List of Illustrations

FOREWORD

by Mark Wilson

In the course of 500 years, the game of golf has provoked a countless variety of emotions. During one of his more irritable moments, George Bernard Shaw declared golf to be a form of 'typical capitalist lunacy,' while Mark Twain condemned it as the means to 'spoil a good walk.' Winston Churchill had the conquering powers to lead the nation to victory in a war, but after a brief flirtation with golf he surrendered with the brusque opinion that 'having to use weapons ill-designed for the purpose' made it an unfair challenge. In contrast, however, Lloyd George discovered that 'You get to know more of the character of a man in a round of golf than you get to know in six months with only political experience.'

Happily, the ranks of respected writers now spreading the gospel of golf throughout the world have been strengthened by Sam Morley whose passion for the game, all the stronger for discovering it comparatively late in life, again makes marvellous reading in *By Yon Bonnie Links!*, his fifth book.

I met Sam – on a golf course, of course – soon after he had been afflicted at the age of 40, due in the first instance to reading Wodehouse and Longhurst, who was also my inspiration as a writer. Sam, whose existence previously had been largely devoted to helping beat Hitler and creating a successful business, then established new priorities by buying a half-set of clubs in a department store, losing his complete stock of 24 golf balls in 10 holes; and immediately heading for an indoor golf school where he registered for 12 lessons.

The pleasures he subsequently discovered travelling and playing golf thankfully encouraged him to share his sense of the ridiculous with everyone as an extremely observant writer. While too many authors presently concern themselves with the ultra serious issues of golf as a potential route to fame and fortune for the gifted, Sam properly appreciates what the game is really about for the vast majority of us – having fun and making friends. And Sam Morley has a lot of both.

July 1990

Editor: Royal and Ancient Club *Golfers Handbook*
Communications Director: PGA European Tour

Previous books by Sam Morley

Start-Off-Smashed!
In Search of Eastern Promise
Victory in 'Site'!
If It Wasn't for Golf . . . !

8

PROLOGUE

I n October 1988, soon after publication of *If It Wasn't For
Golf . . . !* Michael Bonallack – current Secretary of the
Royal and Ancient Golf Club, St Andrews – sent his
congratulations on the book, together with an invitation to
visit and renew old acquaintance when next in the Mecca of
Golf. But not until April of the following year was the offer
taken up and incorporated into a week-long book-
promotion tour through some of Scotland's prestigious
golfing country.

When I was putting the trip together, in which Gleneagles
was the only truly inland objective, the editor of a golfing
magazine suggested that four other Clubs be included on
the grounds that 1989 was their centenary year. That's how
Blairgowrie, Murrayshall, Ranfurly Castle, and Lockerbie
came to be in on the act – although, of course, poor old
Lockerbie had theirs overshadowed by the awful Pan Am
disaster in December 1988.

While on the subject of places featured in this book, the
term Links in the title is 'author's licence', going back to
when it was a generic term used by the uninitiated to mean
a golf course in general. In fact, of the 14 featured only
North Berwick, Musselburgh, St Andrews, Carnoustie,
Prestwick and Troon originate from coastal sand settling

9

down after aeons of battering by wind and water, and allowing a crust of fine turf to form on its surface. The resulting stretch of undulating land – complete with sandy subsoil, erratic water courses, and windswept vegetation – being the essential features of a truly links course.

Using the chosen title rather than *By Six Bonnie Links and Eight Other Scottish Golf Courses* meant cheating a little, but it does run off the tongue better!

At Gleneagles, halfway through the week in question, I bought a copy of *Today's Golfer* in the hotel bookshop. Its editor, Bill Robertson, had negotiated for the rights to feature a chapter from *If It Wasn't For Golf . . . !* in their May issue and somebody at Blairgowrie had mentioned seeing it the previous day.

The magazine had done me proud, with a complete chapter, consisting of a potted biography and anecdotes about Ted Ray – the comic, not the golfer – being given a double-page spread. One of the anecdotes took up almost half the chapter and, by coincidence, was a fascinating story of one of his working holidays at the very place I was currently staying – Gleneagles.

I phoned Bill Robertson from my hotel room to congratulate him on the presentation. When he learned where I was, and why, he was intrigued and wanted to know more. Especially when told I had been at Carnoustie the previous day. 'I was born there!', he said, and went on to suggest my writing an opinionated light-hearted account of the 'passing Scottish show' – with the possibility of its being run in his magazine at some future date.

'About two thousand words would do nicely', was his closing remark.

My third book, *Victory In 'Site'!*, came to be written the same way. A trade magazine asked for about 2,000 words on how folks hunted for their business in the Construction industry, but they never did get it. There proved to be so much to say. It finished up 12 months later as a 65,000-word hardback in the spring of 1987, and is still selling.

And that's how history came to repeat itself. For it wasn't until I started delving into what others had written about an area recognised the world over as the cradle of golf, that a fascinating 250-year old story came to light, thanks to two dedicated researchers digging deeper than their predecessors and publishing some highly colourful information for the first time nine years ago. A story that makes an ideal backdrop against which to tell my own. Once again, however it's going to run to a bit more than 2,000 words.

So, Bill, although it now looks as though you'll never get that magazine article, feel free to reproduce anything that takes your fancy out of here – with the usual credits of course! That's the least I can do, seeing it was your suggestion that 'put the show on the road' in the first place.

1

North Berwick

Phone calls, letters, and sample complimentary copies of the book having been used to prepare the ground, I left home and a sleeping wife at about 6.30 am, with a bag of clothes, a bag of clubs, and 180 copies of *If it wasn't for Golf . . . !* stashed on the back seat and in the boot of my old Rover. Not that I thought the planned programme would allow much time for golf, but that old car won't go anywhere without those clubs in the back. It was Monday, 24 April 1989.

The morning sunshine was blotted out by a blinding snowstorm by the time I'd reached a contraflow shambles on the A1(M) near Doncaster, but had returned in all its glory after a 'full-house' breakfast at a Little Chef 20 miles south of Scotch Corner.

Following the motorway under the Tyne and around the coast past Berwick on Tweed, I entered Scotland on an empty two-lane single carriageway, with the snow-capped Cheviots way out on the left and the North Sea just a couple of hundred yards to the right. And despite media descriptions of that stretch of water as the nation's rubbish tip, there wasn't an empty 'burger-bag or lager-can in sight on its sun-flecked, deep-blue surface. Well, not so much as could be noticed while clocking 70 plus on a winding road.

Despite having visited Scotland many times over the years on business, pleasure, or a bit of each, this was a 'first-timer' into the south-east corner of it. That's probably why the sight of an evocative sign saying 7 miles to North Berwick brought a quick decision to turn right off the A1 for my first non-scheduled stop. Evocative for several reasons.

First, because Paul McGrath, an old pal and fellow past-captain of the Wig and Pen Club, had gone up there to live about 18 months earlier. It would have been a scheduled stop for a few holes and some lunch had he been around, but when discussing our plans over the phone, he said his were to be in the Isle of Wight on an ex-Royal Marine Commando reunion the same week. He happens to be a survivor of that notorious Dieppe raid in summer of '42. A meeting could have been useful as a refresher on that ill-fated exercise, for possible inclusion in a part-written naval book I've been fiddling about with these past five years. But as, once again, that one is relegated to the 'back-burner' due to this one winning 'pole position' (how's that for a mishmash of metaphors!) it'll probably be another five before that story of Paul's gets into print. If ever!

Second, a half set of new left-handed clubs ordered a few months previously from John Hamilton, our pro at Brickendon Grange, came in with the name 'Daiwa' stuck all over them. John assured me that Daiwa was a well-established Japanese business specialising in sports goods, whose golf clubs were made by Ben Sayers, the old-established club-makers of North Berwick.

When putting this story together I was under the impression that Daiwa must have taken over Ben Sayers Ltd – as is the wont of Japanese enterprise with British industry all too often these days – and said as much with woeful pen in the draft pages. But, thankfully, nothing was further from the truth. When I phoned Daiwa at their Ayrshire HQ they explained that sub-contracting to Sayers was only a temporary expedient while they set up their own factory near Kilmarnock. And a three-page story from Paul – who kindly carried out a bit of local research for me on the subject – made it clear that in 100 years of club-making in North Berwick, Ben Sayers Ltd have never had it so good, with its 30,000 square-foot factory currently turning out 4,000 golf clubs a week.

The research also threw up enough colourful background on its founder – a 5'3" North Berwick wag, known universally as the 'Wee Yin' – to justify giving him some mileage in this chronicle.

Ben Sayers was 21 when he played in his first Open Championship at Prestwick in 1875. His partner in the first round was 16-year-old Johnnie Ball from Hoylake who, 15 years later, was the first of only three amateurs ever to win the Open. (The second was Harold Hilton, also from Hoylake, who won it in 1892 and 1897, while the immortal three-timer, Bobby Jones, did it in 1926,1927 and 1930.)

Despite entering every year until 1923, the 'Wee Yin' never did win an Open, but his wit, acrobatic skill and mercurial temperament earned him a lasting reputation as one of the great characters of the game. Had he been playing today he'd have been the darling of TV and of those magazines more taken with colourful human figures than with those written on a scorecard.

It was quite common for him to turn a couple of cartwheels on getting a 'birdie' – with hickory shafts, gutty balls and hand-mown greens, scoring one under par on a hole was not quite as commonplace an achievement then as it is in a big competition today. Probably just as well, as our Open would look like the Bolshoi Ballet on TV, with hefty 'birdie-shooters' – like Trevino, Nicklaus, Lyle and Faldo, to

Ben Sayers – 'The Wee Yin'

name but a few – whirling away like dervishes all over Troon or St George's. The mind boggles!

When a shot of Ben's came to rest high up on the ivy-clad walls of Wemyss Castle while playing in a tournament there, the 'Wee Yin' shinned up the ivy like a squirrel and, hanging on to it with one hand, played an incredible recovery shot with an iron held in the other.

He was a great teacher of the game, with peers, politicians and princes beating a path to the door of his simple shop near the Starter's Box at North Berwick. It was said that if you were lucky enough to get booked into a course of lessons with him you could dine out for a year on stories resulting from the experience. The Czar of Russia sent his son Michael to North Berwick for his golf lessons, and rewarded the 'Wee Yin' with a bolt of pure silk; and presentations were also received from King Edward VII and his grandson George VI when he was Duke of York.

Jack Wallace, a Past President of the Scottish Golf Union and editor of its monthly magazine, *The Scottish Golfer*, told me that his mother lived at Turnberry when she was young. Her father was the hotel electrician and her fiance clubmaker to Tom Fernie, the Club professional. From his mother, Jack learned much of the golfing scene during the early 1900s. When speaking to him about Ben Sayers, he told me of the time she and her sister were involved in providing lunch for Ben and his opponent when they were playing in an all-day exhibition or challenge match out on the course.

Ben came in at the end of the morning round and sat down to eat at the table. Noticing the state of the 'Wee Yin's' hands, Jack's mother suggested he go out and wash them before tucking into the plate of food in front him.

'Na, na, lassie', was the indignant reply, 'I dinna wash ma han's atween roonds. It would spile ma grip for the efternin!'

I sent my draft of this story to Jack in order to get the dialect presentation right. In his reply he said he couldn't recall any other Ben Sayers anecdotes but that one is etched in his memory. He also went on to explain that with the rough grips they had in those days, spitting on the hands combined with the build up of grime through the day would prove quite an advantage.

And now, thanks to the bespoke club-making business he started, Ben's memory stays alive today – and long may it continue to do so. The firm did suggest, however, that with their modern clubs there's little chance of 'spilin' an 'efternin'-grip just through washing off the morning grime before lunch!

North Berwick's 160-year-old golf links has staged tournaments galore and, although consisting of a mere seven holes until 1860, its name crops up continually in stories of golf matches between the giants of yesterday. That was a third reason for my wanting to stop and look around.

With rocky foreshore and pounding ocean forming the boundary to eight of its holes, and still within sight from most of the other ten, it prides itself on being one of the true links courses; that is, created by nature alone as a natural link between land and sea. And as such, many of those natural features have been imitated by others when designing elsewhere.

When Charles Blair Macdonald laid out the US National Golf Course on Long Island in 1907 – rated as one of the world's greatest – he toured the UK in search of what was needed to make each hole an outstanding one. His short 4th he named 'Redan' and built it to match the 15th – and also 'Redan' – at North Berwick. Robert Trent Jones also used 'Redan' when building the 12th at Spyglass Hill, California.

The architect of the Riviera Club, Beverly Hills – once referred to as 'Hogan's Alley' after he'd won three major tournaments there in 18 months – had another North Berwick hole in mind when designing their 6th with a bunker in the middle of the green!

History books tell us that North Berwick is the 13th oldest golf club in the world, and second only to St Andrews in having had continuous play on one site. The Golf Club itself was formed in 1832, but they were hitting balls into holes with sticks along the cliff-tops and down to sandy rock-strewn beaches at North Berwick for two or three hundred years before that. This might be as good a place as any to describe briefly how and where it all started.

In the thirteenth and fourteenth centuries, a game – with sticks shaped very much like our early golf clubs, and feather-stuffed balls – was played around a score or more major cities in Holland. It was called 'Het Kolven', and probably pronounced 'Golffen', as I understand the Dutch introduce a 'gargle' when pronouncing 'K' and sound their 'V's' like an 'f'. Figures carrying and wielding those early clubs are featured in Dutch and Flemish landscape paintings of that era; and researchers have come up with minutes of an Antwerp Town Council meeting in 1927 referring to citizens being exposed to danger through golf fanatics hitting wayward shots. Nothing changes, does it?

The game was first introduced to Britain via the busy Scottish east-coast ports of those days – such as Leith, St Andrews, North Berwick, and Carnoustie. Dutch seamen off vessels plying between the two countries would come ashore in search of fresh air and exercise on the nearest bit of open ground, while awaiting favourable winds for the voyage home. As always, there would have been no shortage of curious onlookers, among whom the more enterprising would have wanted to have a go themselves – and you know how long it takes an enterprising have-a-goer to get himself hooked!

'Het Kolven' eventually died out in Holland, but on that eastern strip of Scottish coast 'The Goff' flourished from the fourteenth century onwards, with open ground close to the sea its natural venue. As the equipment became more sophisticated so did decisions vary on where to cut holes, distances between them, and how many constituted a complete round: all dependent on local conditions and the whims of those playing. It should also be borne in mind that the playing area was on common ground, shared with 'fute'-ballers, archers, soldiers on exercise, fishermen drying nets and housewives drying washing; while hither and yon were groups of children playing their own little games among courting couples playing theirs.

Record books show that five of the six oldest golfing Societies or Clubs still in existence are on the Scottish east coast. These are:

> Royal Burgess Golfing Society of Edinburgh
> Honourable Company of Edinburgh Golfers
> Royal and Ancient Golf Club of St Andrews
> Royal Musselburgh Golf Club
> Bruntsfield Golf Club

Conflicting claims and a surprising paucity of early records cloud their respective ages, although there is no doubt they all came into being somewhere between 1730 and 1780.

But the 'daddy of 'em all' was the south-east London club of Royal Blackheath. It was when writing its history that the authors discovered why all those Scottish societies could not provide accurate details of their origin. That's explained in the next chapter, but here's how 'The Goff' first came south.

When James VI of Scotland became James I of England in 1603, he brought his full Scottish court to London with him. There were thousands of 'em! Fifty leading courtiers are named in the history of Royal Blackheath, but each came with a large retinue of family, servants, retainers, and troops of personal men-at-arms – or 'minders' in today's parlance. Remember, the Scots – and their forebears, the Picts – were never all that popular in the South and 1,500 years earlier the Roman emperor, Hadrian, had a fortified wall built from the Solway to the Tyne to keep them out. Eighty miles long and up to twenty feet thick in places, it lasted a bit longer than the Berlin Wall, but went the same way in the end.

Aware of their semi-hostile surroundings, those addicted to 'The Goff' among the newcomers wasted little time in searching for somewhere to have a knock among themselves while waiting for the natives to get friendlier. The nearest bit of open land to Greenwich Palace was Black Heath, where those early Scottish addicts must have had their first holes cut before their Fife-based removal trucks had finished unloading! But more of all that in the next chapter.

Returning to North Berwick, the exclusive Club of that name, dating back to 1836, is just a Clubhouse. It does not have a golf course of its own – only the right to play and alternate with the playing public on the prestigious West Links, owned and maintained by the East Lothian District Council. Play was prohibited on Sundays, although allowed on the adjoining East Links. But that – as with the Old Course at St Andrews – was said to be more a case of resting the precious turf from the bashing received on the other six days than an effort aimed at getting the ungodly addicts into a church. Or so claimed the godly members of those in power. However, it is now a few years since the turf was considered to be robust enough to stand up to the full seven-day treatment and Sundays are now play-days at West Links, just as they are in most other parts of the land.

The handsome two-storey Clubhouse sits close to the road by the western perimeter of the course, and was once 'out-of-bounds' to all but members and their personal guests. But the Club now manages the course for the District Council, and once visitors have paid their West Links green fee at the Starter's Box they are considered to have qualified for day membership of the Club, whereby changing facilities, dining room, and bar are all at their disposal. Neither is there any discrimination as far as ladies are concerned – which is more than can be said about a number of other Clubs featured in this book.

But golf is a way of life in so many other parts of Scotland, where it is normal to arrive at the first tee suitably dressed for playing, having previously booked a time to do so over the telephone, and to pay a green fee at the Starter's Box close by. Should food or drink be wanted after the game, it's just a matter of finding the nearest café, pub or hotel that can provide it. All the green fee buys is a ticket allowing a player to knock a ball around as many of the available holes as suits the purpose.

As North Berwick's golf links are owned by the local authority and designated public land, visitors would be well advised to avoid school holidays when planning a visit – there being no shortage of children, or adults, wending their way across fairways and playing areas to their favourite spots along the rock-strewn beaches.

Patric Dickinson, in his most informative but highly amusing book, *A Round of Golf Courses*, describes the scene on North Berwick's West Links:

Pedestrians and Equestrians – 'the warp of the tapestry of which golfers are the woof!'

Bass Rock towers over Redan bunker-play. *(Photo: E. Danks and Son, North Berwick)*

The first hole sets the tone. It is a mad hole, anyway. Across its expanse pass, in endless rout, the holiday columns attacking the sea; backwards and forwards they go – the warp of a tapestry of which we golfers are the woof . . .

Over the first three holes there is no shot that is not observed and mocked by young men and maidens, old men and children . . .

Although this absorbing book was published in 1951, I understand little has changed from Mr Dickinson's observation.

Neither does he agree with American architects that 'Redan', the short 15th, is a great one, and wonders what other short holes they must have seen and rejected in its favour. 'It looks nice,' he writes, 'but rather artificial.' He thought that might have been the endearing factor to American golf architects, who

seem to love 'folding' and 'moulding'; and would like to do their work in some substance like plastic and put out whole links in pre-fabricated slabs. Whereby huge concrete casts of 'The Redan' may be used all over the States and covered with earth, sand, turf, and the like . . .

He goes on to provide details of some of the more unusual holes, but excels with his description of the eighteenth:

and from the last tee a cut drive can earn immortality by denting a Rolls-Royce. All along the right is the road where you park your car; but there is a world of room to the left with the chance of denting any number of holiday-makers, or even players who have so far only hit one blow.

Finally, although I said earlier this was my first time in that corner of the country, North Berwick was a name known only too well to me from my personal 'War-at-Sea'. From where I stood near the Clubhouse, two distinctive islands – links with those grim, bygone days – stood out bright and clear in the spring sunshine: Bass Rock and May Island. They brought back harsh memories of 20 months spent on a V & W destroyer nearly 50 years earlier, escorting huge convoys of merchant ships to and from the Thames and Channel ports.

Steaming downstream from our base at Rosyth, we'd do a 'one-man-and-his-dog' round-up at the convoy assembly-point off Methil, on the north bank of the Forth, and proceed out of the estuary exchanging greetings, signals and curses with up to a hundred ships of varying size, speed, cargo, and nationality. Curses usually reserved for the black-smoke-makers, sluggards and wanderers. Sticking carefully to the mine-swept channel, once the convoy crossed a line drawn between North Berwick and May Island it changed course for a 60-hour southbound zig-zag run to Sheerness at the mouth of the Thames.

And once Bass Rock was on the port beam at the end of a northbound run – usually every bit as traumatic as the one down had been – it was time to get the No.1 suit out for an airing, ready for a run ashore on completion of the final 25 miles into Rosyth dockyard. There were of course times when those suits were crammed back hurriedly into lockers, unworn, due to a signal ordering us to double up for a destroyer in the 'next shift' that had 'blown a gasket' or hit a mine. In such cases we'd have to top up quickly with fuel and ammo before belting back to Methil – where an assembled Southbound convoy was apprehensively waiting to start out for 'E-boat Alley' and the usual 'ticker-tape' reception by bomb-happy Heinkels, Junkers, Dorniers and Messerschmitts!

But as all that was a long time ago and nothing whatever to do with Golf, let's return to 1989. Anybody wanting to know more about those halcyon wartime days will have to wait until the next book's into print. Called *Ninety Years of Navy*, it's about 30 per cent written, but with all this demand for the golfing scene Lord alone knows when that other 70 per cent will see the light of day.

David Huish, the North Berwick professional, commenting on the latent demand in and around his Club for good quality books with a witty golfing theme, complained of a shop heavily stocked with golfing merchandise for the start of the season with nobody as yet showing much interest. But he did promise to get an order off as soon as enough shoes, putters, sweaters, gloves, matched sets of clubs and the like had been bought off his shelves. *(Must have had a bad season as nothing's arrived so far.)*

2

Muirfield

A few miles along the coast brought me to Muirfield, the celebrated home of the Honourable Company of Edinburgh Golfers. When planning the trip I had asked the Secretary over the phone if their professional might like to stock *I.I.W.F.G* in his shop, especially as Chapter 5 told how the Horrible Company of Cambridge Golfers chose its name after traumatic experiences at Muirfield. He was curious about that, but made it clear that neither golf professionals nor their shops played any part in the make-up of his historic establishment.

The reason was one of economics. Most members of the Hon. Golfers were also members of other Clubs nearer their homes – in and around Edinburgh – where all the equipment and lessons they fancied could be bought. There was not enough regular traffic at Muirfield to employ a full-time pro, except at weekends and during the height of the season. In 1928, Jack White – an ex-Sunningdale professional who won the Open in 1904 – asked if he could start a shop at Muirfield. After much deliberation the Committee agreed, with the proviso that he didn't sell golf balls! That had long been the established 'perks' of the Club steward and Muirfield was the last place to ride roughshod over established patronage and tradition.

" Sorry, no chips - but I can do you
a dozen golf balls with your haddock "

Jack withdrew his application – well, a pro shop barred from selling golf balls is like a fried fish shop barred from selling chips – but was allowed to set up a temporary shop on the course when Championship meetings were held. The pro at nearby Gullane took over the concession once Jack retired.

Without a shop that might be persuaded to stock my books, there wasn't much point in calling into Muirfield – especially as the programme was already crowded. But to satisfy the Secretary's ill-concealed curiosity about the Horrible Company of Cambridge Golfers, I sent him a complimentary copy of *If it wasn't for Golf . . . !* with a covering note, and received a nice letter of appreciation by return; also an invitation to call at another time more suitable to my plans.

But now, passing the door so to speak, and having made far better time than anticipated – thereby having a couple of hours to spare before my first scheduled appointment – a visit and look round was too good to miss.

Finding the place was the first problem. Just as nowhere around London can a sign be seen pointing to Buckingham Palace, there was nothing on the highways or byways of Muirfield or Gullane to tell a stranger in which direction lay the hallowed portals of the Honourable Company of Edinburgh Golfers. Directions had to be asked of three different villagers before their combined instructions brought me to the three-storey Clubhouse at the end of a quiet residential road. Even so, it could just as easily have been a private nursing home, a training college for rising ICI executives, or the HQ of Sheikh Abdullah's racing stables – for there was still no indication of who lived there.

Gordon Vanreenen, the Club Secretary, had his office door open and my book on his desk when I entered, although he was quite surprised at being visited by its author when he had a letter saying otherwise beside it. Had *By Yon Bonnie Links!*

been envisaged at the time I could have well spent a couple of hours there gathering background material, and saved weeks and weeks of poring over old reference books trying to trace the history of this time-encrusted establishment.

But by dint of burning a few gallons of midnight oil over the said old books, a hitherto little-publicised piece of history is here brought to light and offered as a stimulating newsflash. On second thoughts hardly a flash, as it does go on a bit. But there's no doubt about the news-content in what follows, once the scene-setting preamble is over.

When a group of addicts, calling themselves The Gentlemen Golfers of Edinburgh, had the Lord Provost of the City put up a Silver Club as a prize for a golfing competition in 1744, they were asked to prepare a set of playing rules for the said event. Quite a project, as it was the first golfing competition ever recorded in world history. It was also quite an achievement, as their 13 Rules of Golf – passed en bloc to the Society of St Andrews Golfers when they in turn got themselves together for a competition with a Silver Club as a prize ten years later – have changed very little over the ensuing 246 years. Contrary to popular belief the Rules for the actual competition were not drawn up by the Hon. Golfers but by the Edinburgh Town Council, and are reproduced in full from the Council Minutes in Chapter 4.

The winner of that first contest was given the title 'Captain of the Golf' for a year and, at the dinner that followed, a silver golf ball with his name inscribed on it was attached to the club. Since then and on taking office, each successive Captain has done likewise. When no room remained on the club for further balls, somebody whispered into the Lord Provost's ear (well, no doubt he was a past-Captain anyway) and the City would come up with another Silver Club. They are now working on their fourth Silver

Club up at Muirfield, although when the competition started the Hon. Golfers played their golf on the public course at Leith Links – as did Mary, Queen of Scots, a couple of hundred years earlier. (But it was at Seton House that she was seen having a knock too soon after the untimely death of her husband, Lord Darnley. He was said to have been blown up by a jealous suitor when sleeping off a touch of the 'lurgies', while Mary was out attending the wedding of one of her staff.)

Reverting to golfbook instead of schoolbook-history, it was not until long after starting research for the background to this story that I came across some surprising information; little known, it would seem, by almost all who'd written knowledgeably on the subject for 200 years before 1981. But first a brief digression.

David White is one of four enthusiasts who founded the British Golf Collectors Society, and produces, single-handed, their quarterly magazine. I've known him since 1974 when, as curator of a St Andrews Museum, he said nice things about my first book, *Start-Off-Smashed!*, to a friend browsing around the shelves when a wet and windy day kept him off the course. Soon after *If It Wasn't for Golf* was published David wrote glowing reviews in each of the two magazines he then edited.

Needing advice on the best books for the early history of Scottish east-coast Links and Clubs to help me with this story, I couldn't think of a better source of information. He reminded me that a promised visit to his home in Seaford, East Sussex, was long overdue, as was a game at his local Club, and I knew that he'd be happy to lend me whatever was needed from the hundreds of golfing books lining his shelves.

He wasn't exaggerating either, I found, when being shown round his golfing 'museum' one sunny day about a month before Christmas 1989. Every corner of the house was used to display golfing memorabilia to its best advantage, but nothing detracted from the fact that it was still a warm and tastefully-furnished home. His wife, Ursula, provided us with lunch while we discussed the seven books he had on the table ready for me to take away. After that we played 14 holes on Seaford Golf Club's panoramic sea-girt course, some 500 yards from his home.

It was also one of those rare occasions when I've been able to try another's clubs during a round, we both being left-handed. Although with true one-upmanship, and as an afficionado of every aspect of the game, he didn't believe in playing with 'store-bought' clubs – just built his own for 'kicks' in his garage-cum-workshop. I soon found it was just as easy to mishit with a David White special as with a Daiwa assembly-line model.

Six of the books he'd selected were to fill me in on the Clubs I'd spoken about, but the seventh contained the surprise element and was not to be opened until all had been sucked and digested from the others. From the first six – as from many previously read – it was clear that 'the Goff' was a popular pastime along that east coast from 1350 onwards for those who could afford the costly feather-stuffed balls and weirdly-shaped sticks. So popular was it that in 1457, 1471, and again in 1491, successive monarchs felt obliged to pass laws banning it on the grounds that, 'fute-ball, golf, and other sik unprofitable sports distracted young men from archery exercise and church attendance'. (As no doubt it does today. Ask around and find out how many in your Club have fired an arrow or been to Matins since taking up the game!)

But even after those laws were repealed in 1502 there is no record of groups being formed to play competitions and make merry after their game, until those Honourable Golfers went 'pot-hunting' 242 years later.

They celebrate 1744 as the date of the first-ever organised golf event and the founding date of their Society – later to become the Honourable Company of Edinburgh Golfers. But where did they all come from to enter for that event and justify their high-sounding title?

Patric Dickinson, whom I quote on North Berwick in the previous chapter almost came up with the answer in 1951 when writing of Muirfield. He quotes some lines from 'The Goff, 1743', in which the poet lyrically describes the scene on Leith Links, naming many of the players and their individual styles of play. Referring to the poet, Dickinson goes on:

but he was not one of the select band of 'Gentleman Golfers' who met at Mrs. Clephan's tavern on play-days at Leith and drank deeply of claret after their games. These gentlemen golfers were a 'club', that is , a group well in the habit of meeting together well before 1744 . . . .

Whatever its intentions, the competition was a closed event, confined to the Gentleman Golfers.

But it was that seventh book that produced a simple answer to the 250-year-old mystery and clearly defined the nature and workings of that 'club'.

Royal Blackheath, by Ian Thomson Henderson, CBE, MA, and David Stirk, FRCS, was published under their own imprint in 1981. In its opening chapter they go into great detail of how King James brought his favourite game and an entourage of thousands to London with him in 1603, as described earlier. Chapter Two is headed, 'The Organisation by Scottish Freemasons of the early Golfing Societies'.

Why is it, inferred the joint authors, that so many other kinds of old establishments, going back hundreds of years before the period we're talking about, still have intact records; but in every case when investigating the beginnings of organised golf, such minute books as could be unearthed had their opening pages torn out or mutilated? Yes, even Blackheath's. But the job wasn't done too well in the case of the latter, and some pages were only partially damaged. From what was left and after much clinical 'pathology' on the Scottish records, entries and references were traced relating to rituals, initiations, uniforms, dining commitments, 'Bett books', and names or initials of individuals prefixed by 'Brother' or 'MM' (Master Mason). The authors were thus able to see a completely new logical picture of how those Societies got off the ground. To quote:

> Golf was not the primary objective and it was groups of Scottish Freemasons who adopted it as a healthy form of exercise prior to their feasting and were thus responsible for the earliest form of organised golf. The systematic destruction of early minutes has successfully concealed the fact for over two hundred years.

The purpose of this wanton destruction, implied the book, was to conceal their 'secrets' (rituals) from non-Masons, who were allowed to infiltrate the Societies when the movement waned during the nineteenth century. Organised Freemasonry, as represented by Grand Lodge presided over by a Grand Master and a number of private lodges, was started in Scotland in 1736 – just eight years before the Hon. Company played their first competition – and William St Clair of Roslin is recorded as the first Grand Master of the Scottish Grand Lodge. (He is also recorded as four-times Captain of the Hon. Golfers. His portrait, with the exaggerated closed stance, hangs in the Clubhouse at Muirfield and is ghosted on the back of the jacket to this book.) A few years later his name is given as the central figure at a Masonic ceremony staged by the Hon. Golfers.

But to return for the moment to the Gentlemen Golfers and that first competition in 1744. In order to justify expenditure of public money on a golf prize the City Council had ruled that the contest be open to all; not just among the members of a closed shop, so to speak, that happened to play the game.

Not until 1764, when the Gentlemen, or Hon. Golfers, first drew up their Rules of Membership, did they obtain permission to continue the fixture as an 'in-house' affair among its own members. Having no accommodation at Leith they then decided to build a 'Golfing House', to be rented to a tenant on the understanding that the Hon. Golfers had the exclusive use of it for their own fixtures. The book quotes a minute of 2 July 1768 as follows:

This day William St Clair of Roslin Esquire, the Undoubted representative of the honourable and heritable G.M.M. of Scotland In the presence of Alexander Keith Esquire Captain of the honourable company of Golfers and other worthy members of the Golfing Company, all Masons . . . laid the foundation stone of the Golfing House in the S.E. Corner thereof by THREE STROKES with the MALLETT.

The minute goes on to name the 12 other members present and the Masonic rank of each. From the previous paragraph and the above minute it would appear that the Golfing Society, as opposed to miscellaneous members of a Masonic lodge hooked on the game, really started in 1764 – not 1744 as they claim – and went on to build its own Clubhouse by the side of the public links four years later. It is also interesting to note that the above William St Clair, Grand Master Mason of Scottish Grand Lodge, had already been Captain of the Hon. Company in 1761, and was again installed in 1766, 1770 and 1771.

From the foregoing emerges a far clearer picture of how it all started. By inventing fictitious characters and dialogue – much the same as Shakespeare did to teach us English and Roman history in the making – here, with all due respect, although with a slightly irreverent touch, is how I see the origins of the Honourable Company of Edinburgh Golfers.

Picture the scene in an Edinburgh Masonic temple, with the brethren arriving from their worldly affairs and donning aprons, sashes, etc., in preparation for one of their pre-1744 lodge meetings. Brother Campbell looks across at Brother Walker and says … (*not being in Shakespeare's class I'll stick to the language of today rather than dabble in flowery phrases of the period*):

'Didn't I see you playing Goff with Brother Grant yesterday on the links at Leith? I was in a three-ball just behind, having a knock with my lawyer and one of his partners.'

'Yes, I thought I recognised you, but it was a bit misty and the rain didn't help. Hope we didn't hold you up when my ball went out of bounds on the third.'

'Not at all. How about us finding two and making up a four next Thursday?'

'Good idea! But I should warn you I'm on form at the moment. Went round in 37 yesterday.' [*Remember, there were only five holes at Leith – but all over 400 yards.*]

Overhearing all this from an adjacent locker, Brother Duncan speaks up. 'Wouldn't mind giving either of you a game myself some time. Did a 35 last week and 34 a couple of weeks back. Be a good idea if we had a competition among those Lodge members who play and the one who wins most holes wins the prize.'

'What prize?'

'Well, the Worshipful Master's been on to the Lord Provost of the City for the past year or so to put up a prize for such a competition, but he's not having any. Says something about the Links belonging to the public in general and he can't justify spending public money on a prize for golfing Freemasons only.'

Just then, in walks the Worshipful Master. 'Sorry I'm a bit late, chaps, but I've just come from lunching with the Lord Provost. Over the second decanter we finally got it all tied up. What do you want first – the good news or the bad?'

'Let's start with the good,' was the general cry.

'Well, you know we've some budding "William Tells" in the Lodge that call themselves the Honourable Archers of Edinburgh – a menace to all and sundry when firing arrows down at Leith. Back in 1709 the City Council presented them with a Silver Arrow to be shot for annually at the Links. I've been complaining to the Lord Provost for some time about the City Fathers favouring the archers in preference to golfers, and the penny's finally dropped.

'The City of Edinburgh has now agreed to put up a Silver Golf Club as a prize for a competition at The Goff, to be played over Leith Links one year from today. The Silver Club is to be presented to the player winning most holes over three rounds. The winner's name is to be engraved on a silver ball, to be hung from the Club, and the trophy displayed in a safe place. The competition is to be held again the following year, and the presentation with another engraved silver ball to be made by the Lord Provost at a suitably ceremonial banquet.'

Loud cheers all round. Cries of 'Good old W.M.!!' Then: 'What about the bad news?'

'Ah, I was just coming to that. To justify the expenditure it has to be a competition open to all that regularly use the Links. And to let justice be seen to be done he's going to get the Town Crier to march around the Links on the day before the competition, preceded by a pair of blokes beating a drum or blowing a trumpet, announcing a contest on the morrow over 15 holes, in which all may take part on payment of an entrance fee of five shillings. Can't see many drovers, churls or crossing-sweepers putting up a month's pay just for the privilege of having a trophy with their name on it hanging up in the City Hall, or some other place – like perhaps a Masonic temple, if you get my drift!'

'He said that as there's no record of anything like this ever being done before', went on the Worshipful Master, 'he wants us to draw up a set of playing rules so that everybody competes on equal terms. During which time he'll get some prices from the silversmiths. That is once we've given him a design for the club they're to make.

'When I told him that we always played in our Masonic uniforms, so that all could note we were the élite and not part of the *hoi polloi* that all too often clutter up the Links and hinder the recreation of gentlemen, he raised no objection to our doing so on this occasion and thought it would help enhance the overall scene. He said that once we'd got ourselves a proper set of rules – Society rules, that is, not the golfing ones we've got to have ready for the competition – and a clearly defined Society membership, it might be possible to phase out the open nature of the event and make it an exclusive one for our members only. But it'll probably take us a few years to build up acceptance as a *bona-fide* Golfing Society, independent of Masonic activities and with its own Captain and Committee. Which means that once recognised as such up at City Hall, we'll probably be allowed to keep the Silver-Club-and-Ball ritual going as our own perks – after all we are the ones entrusted with getting it all started for them – and the City will put up another trophy as an open thing for the 'proles' on the Links.'

And Lo, in the fullness of time, so it all came to pass! The story of Golf and Freemasonry is a fascinating one. To anyone interested in following it through, the book in question, *Royal Blackheath*, was still available from that Club when this chapter was compiled late in 1989.

One of the many links between Golf and 'The Square' is an obsession to reward achievements in Freemasonary with decorations that can be worn with the lodge regalia. Such an achievement – or execution of a particular duty – is often recognised with the traditional presentation of a medal. As a result a good Mason with a few years of service could often look as resplendent as a Christmas tree when decked out in his full regalia. When competitive Golf emanated from the Masonic lodges, what could be more in keeping with usual practice than to reward a good performance with the presentation of a medal? And right to this day, the basic and oldest-established competition in almost every Golf Club is . . . the Monthly Medal!

Only in most of the Clubs I know they don't serve out medals any more. They just present an apostle tea-spoon and cut a couple of shots off the poor devil's handicap.

(Many of the old Clubs and Societies in Scotland, including Muirfield, Royal Burgess, and at least four others in this book, still do not allow ladies in their premises – except once or twice a year at special functions – another spin-off from established Masonic practice.)

In March 1800, the Honourable Golfers of Edinburgh were granted a charter by the City and became The Honourable Company of Edinburgh Golfers.

The Society prospered through the early part of the nineteenth century, but things started to deteriorate and money trouble accumulated through unpaid subs, poor attendances at the post-play dinners, and an absconding secretary. They were forced to borrow, using the Clubhouse as collateral, and the building finally had to be sold by public auction because they couldn't raise enough cash to pay interest on the loan. That was in 1834, two years after its contents had been auctioned for a mere £106 in a vain attempt to keep the bailiffs at bay.

This didn't mean that the Society was defunct – just broke and without a base HQ at Leith; where it was getting a bit crowded anyway. The crowd scene is described for us by Thomas Smollett, a Scottish novelist, in a series of letters entitled *Humphrey Clinker* and written in 1771, the year he died:

. . . in the fields called the Links, the citizens of Edinburgh direct themselves at a game called golf, in which they use curious kind of bats tipt with horn, and small elastic balls of leather, stuffed with feathers, rather less than tennis balls, but of a much harder consistence – these they strike with such force and dexterity from one hole to another that they will fly to an incredible distance. Of this diversion the Scots are so fond that when the weather will permit, you will see a multitude of all ranks, from the senator of justice to the lowest tradesmen, mingled together in their shirts, and following the ball with the utmost eagerness. Among others I was shown one particular set of golfers the youngest of whom was turned of four-score. They were all gentlemen of independent fortunes, who had amused themselves with this pastime for the best part of a century without ever having ever felt the least alarm from sickness or disgust [in those days another term for nausea], and they never went to bed without having each the best part of a gallon of claret in his belly.

It sounds as though old Smollett found the forebears of some of the characters haunting midweek fairways of most Clubs today.

Being now without a Golf-house and reluctant to go on sharing Leith with the ever-increasing plebeian crowds, in 1836 the Honourable Company decided to switch their venue to the old nine-hole public links at Musselburgh, on the banks of the Forth estuary and 6 miles east of Edinburgh. Nevertheless they still had to go on sharing with Musselburgh Golf Club, The Burgess Golfers, Bruntsfield Golfing Society (of all of which more later) plus smaller societies and numerous itinerant hackers. And in the fullness of time they again built themselves a Golfing-house on the edge of the links.

The world's first Open Golf Championship was played at Prestwick in 1860 as the Championship Belt (see Chapter 16) and remained there as its annual venue for the next ten years. Prestwick had proposed the Championship be held alternately at Prestwick and St Andrews, and offered to help with the prize in 1856. But St Andrews showed no more than lukewarm enthusiasm and, in the end, Prestwick decided to go it alone: it bought the Belt and organised the competition on its own ground.

In 1868, 1869 and 1870 the Belt was won by Tom Morris, Jnr. A condition of the contest was that anybody winning it three years in succession kept the Belt. Thus, in 1871, no Belt being available, no competition was held.

By this time, no doubt, the century-old clubs and Societies on the east coast of Scotland had woken to the fact that what was fast becoming a prestigious national event was entrenched in a mere 20-year-old private Club in the west. After much negotiation it was agreed, in time for the 1872 Open to be played again at Prestwick, that St Andrews would stage it in 1873 and the Hon. Golfers at Musselburgh in 1874: and thereafter in rotation – all three having chipped in to buy the trophy, a silver Claret Cup. (Another interesting link with the 'drinking Masons' is the choice of a Claret Cup.)

Come 1892 the Honourable Company brought about the eternal displeasure of their erstwhile friends at Musselburgh. Tired again of sharing the use of public links with all and sundry, they had acquired some land out at Muirfield, 15 miles from Edinburgh, and got old Tom Morris, professional at St Andrews and four times winner of the Open in the 1860s, to come over and lay out a brand-new 18-hole playground for them.

With their new course not yet a year old and hardly suitable, they turned their back on Musselburgh and insisted on having its turn at the Open played at Muirfield in 1892. It was a far from popular decision, and players blamed poor scoring on the condition of a course hacked out of virgin territory and not yet a year old.

J.H. Taylor, who won the Open five times over the ensuing 20 years, though never at Muirfield, wrote that the course was never fit to be the home of so great a Club. And even in 1966, when the rough at Muirfield was allowed to grow unkempt and high for the Open, Doug Sanders remarked he'd rather have the hay concession than the prize money!

So here we find an old-established Golfing Society becoming a self-contained Golf Club in the full meaning of the word for the first time in 1892. Sure, they drew up the first set of rules on how the game should be played in 1744, but they were then just some addicted members of a Masonic lodge indulging in their favourite pastime and sharing a public park with others in order to do so. This they continued to do while their fortunes peaked and waned over the next 147 years, until they set up their own private playground at Muirfield in 1891.

They've every right to be proud of their archaic beginnings but nobody would think any the less of them if they played down the pomposity and switched the name to Muirfield Golf Club. They could always add – 'Home of the Honourable Company of Edinburgh Golfers'. And with royal patronage granted by King George VI in 1937 – he having been an Honorary Life Member of the Club since 1929 – they might even be allowed the title of 'Royal Muirfield'.

The self-importance encountered at Muirfield is without parallel. Stories to illustrate this are legion, of which the following – told to me in a bar at St Andrews – is an example:

A senior member of an exclusive South Carolina country club, on a golfing tour across Scotland, called at Muirfield to ask if he might play a round on payment of a green fee.

'Not without an acceptable letter of introduction', was the Secretary's terse response. (Not the current Major, I hasten to add, although ex-Service eminence seems to be a pre-requisite for would-be Secretaries of prestigious golf Clubs.)

'I've got that right here', said the enthusiastic Southerner, 'and it's signed by my ole buddy, our Club President back home.'

Gingerly accepting the proffered sheet of paper the Secretary gave it one cursory glance before letting it flutter to the floor.

'This is no use to me!' he told his bewildered visitor.

The man bent to pick up the paper and started to read aloud: 'To whom it may concern. This is to introduce . . . '

'That is unacceptable as a letter of introduction', broke in the other, 'I am no "to-whom-it-may-concern". I . . . [pause for effect] . . . am the Secretary of the Honourable Company of Edinburgh Golfers!'

(Shouldn't be a bit surprised if poor ole 'South Carolina' was made to write that final sentence 100 times before being allowed to play the course.)

On the other hand, I'm given to understand that they've a refreshing sense of humour there and any amount of these 'Pooh Bah' stories start in their own bar. Somebody sees the Sec. approaching, pulls his leg over an imaginary person getting 'the elbow' there yesterday in keeping with the Club's reputation, and the story is pushed around among the members present and embellished before being allowed to circulate as, 'You heard what happened up at Muirfield last week?'

They also have a wild-and-woolly reputation to live up to, if a 200-year-old set of Bett-Book entries relating to some of the wagers made during those ancient après-golf dinners is anything to go by. The examples given are from the Royal Blackheath book, as those in George Pottinger's *Muirfield and the Honourable Company* are not so high-spirited; but there's little doubt those old east coast Masonic golfers carried on in much the same way as their ex-Scottish cousins in the South.

The date at the end of each wager is the year of entry in the Betts-Book, and a gallon of claret or whisky was usually the stake between a pair of named diners, with them each backing personal prowess or opinion against the other's. Be it on golf or:

1   Whether it was lawful to buy and sell shares after a dividend had been declared. (1791)
2   The specific day in April the island of Tobago in the Caribbean had been captured from the French. (1793)
3   Whether diner A would beat diner B when playing with one hand and receiving a stroke a hole. [He did!] (1825)
4   Whether diner C would beat diner D when playing with a quart bottle, teeing his ball up each time where it came to rest, and having two strokes for one. [He did, too!] (1824)
5   Whether Nelson would intercept the French fleet before they made port in France or America. [He did too!] (1805)
6   Whether diner E would make good his boast and snap a broomstick suspended between two bumpers of wine without spilling a drop or breaking a glass. [The book said he didn't and it lost him a gallon of claret.] (1822)

[Not a word about who cleared the shattered glass off the wine-soaked table cloth!]

Still, it's great golfing country around Muirfield and Gullane with no less than six courses left to choose from – even if you don't have the right credentials for *persona grata* treatment by the Honourable Company of Edinburgh Golfers.

In his Foreword to George Pottinger's excellent book *'Muirfield and the Honourable Company*, Lord Robertson, Senator of the College of Justice and Captain of the Hon. Company, 1969–72, quotes: 'for Muirfield is a place that loves to be visited'. I just wonder if 'ole South Carolina' – or the Cambridge group whose story appears at the end of Chapter 4 – would go along with that one.

That, I believe, is the same Lord Robertson who was one of the judges in the case of Patrick Meehan, sentenced to life imprisonment for murder. Meehan was granted a Royal Pardon after Ludovic Kennedy, the celebrated author and television personality, wrote *A Presumption of Innocence* in a successful campaign to overturn their lordships' ruling. Ludovic Kennedy was black-balled when proposed for membership of Muirfield some time afterwards. When interviewed, he was reported as saying:

> One or two members have indicated that the lawyers at Muirfield took it as an attack on their profession as a whole. Lord Robertson, who was a judge in the second half of the Meehan case, is also a former captain of the Club.
>
> But my criticisms were not personal – they were professional. We Scots are a slightly different breed. We are over-sensitive to criticism and tend to take things personally.

One wonders how those over-sensitive 'legal-eagles' at Muirfield must have reacted when fellow-member George Pottinger – he with the splendid two-storey villa beside Muirfield's first fairway and a newly-published history of his famous Club – involved the said Club in much unsavoury publicity when – with John Poulson, the Architect – he was joint central figure in a *cause célèbre* of the 1970s.

Those sensitive legal-eagles must also have taken exception to the implications of a newspaper interview with George Pottinger, where he was reported as saying that, 'with the influence of those around him he would never have been charged, let alone face a marathon criminal trial, if the police investigation had not been ordered from London'.

A highly-erudite and charismatic character, he has long since left both villa and company of the Honourable Golfers, to live and write among the Sassenachs.

David Stirk, co-author of the *Royal Blackheath* book and many other works on golfing history, was sent an early draft of this chapter for comment on the accuracy of some of my conclusions. When returning it he drily commented at the foot of a page of helpful notes: 'This is good breezy stuff (though whether you will ever be allowed to play at Muirfield again after publication is an interesting question!)'

Be that as it may, I have thoroughly enjoyed the weeks spent in researching and preparing this – the longest and what I believe to be one of the most fascinating chapters in the book.

And to round off my story of this great Club with a light observation on the love/hate relationship we each have with this game of Golf, the final paragraph of George Pottinger's *Muirfield and The Honourable Company* credits Lord Robertson with a reminder to aspiring champions that, 'My favourite shots are the practice swing and the conceded putt – the rest can never be mastered!'

3

Musselburgh Links

D riving westward along the scenic coast road for 12 miles brought me to Musselburgh. Once again it wasn't on the itinerary but I was glad to stop and take a look at what was left of the Old Links course.

How important that little town must have felt a hundred years earlier, rising in esteem as Leith fell from favour, hosting the increasingly popular Open Championship every three years, with more and more spin-off commercial enterprises settling round-and-about because of the expanding potential.

Sic transit gloria Musselburgh!

When I found what was left of the links in and among the racecourse scene about a mile east of the town, it could well have been the backdrop to Act Two of 'Sleeping Beauty' – a racecourse-dominated site enshrouding a once-bustling nine-hole golf course, waiting for some Prince Charming to arrive, dust it off, give it a kiss, and spend a few bob on restoring it to its past elegance for all to enjoy. A veritable golfing time-warp.

Dotted around were derelict remains of Golf-houses belonging to the great exclusive Societies of yesterday – the former links-side bases, built by and reserved for Edinburgh's élite, whose members jostled with each other for the privilege of being given the next available slot on the first tee. Societies such as the Royal Musselburgh, Burgess Golfing Society of Edinburgh, Bruntsfield Links, Honourable Company of Edinburgh Golfers – the very 'Founding Fathers' of the game. Yet they were without identification marks or plates other than the letters BLGC (Bruntsfield Links Golf Club) engraved on a stone panel in the front wall of one of them. But when the Hon. Company took it into its head to move up the coast to Muirfield in 1892, as described in the last chapter, it pulled the rug out from under those that remained and, as they each in turn rolled up their tent and did likewise, the old time-encrusted links went into a long, lingering decline. Royal Musselburgh today has its own 18-hole parkland course about a mile away, designed by James Braid in the 1930s, as was the 18-holes of Musselburgh Golf Club at nearby Monktonhall. The Burgess had theirs laid out at Barnton on the west side of Edinburgh by Tom Morris in 1885, as did Bruntsfield Links in 1897 by Willie Park.

Which left old Musselburgh Links nursing the only nine truly-links holes in the area and wondering where everybody had gone.

Well, there you have the effects of public ownership. Run by a District Council with a vested interest in the development of a race course and indifferent to the maintenance of a golf one, the Links was losing its appeal even before the Hon. Company departed in 1892. The uncontrolled traffic of an ever-increasing army of hackers, horses, and holiday-makers made it more and more difficult for a golfing addict to get round. But in its heyday, about the time of that first Open at Prestwick in 1860, the trains used to steam into Musselburgh from Edinburgh crowded with addicts, their eager caddies waiting on the platform to grab the clubs of their favourites and hurry to the line of horse-drawn cabs queueing at the station entrance. Then would start a mad dash to the Links, each cabbie straining to get his fare to the Starter's Box ahead of the others – thereby qualifying for a bit over the odds when it came to paying whatever was 'on the clock'!

Ball-makers, club-makers, gimmick-makers, professionals and other spin-off entrepreneurs of the game set up shop in and around the town, and many of its citizens set out to preach the word of Golf to the 'Ungolfly' around the world. It was the birthplace of golf as a business. They didn't do too badly at it either from what can be seen of things today. Every schoolboy was a caddy – many went on to win the Open later.

But as the action drifted away to pastures new, little interest was shown by the District Council in cleaning up and retaining the glory-that-was-Musselburgh on sentimental or historic grounds, let alone for the national pride that's supposed to burn fiercely in the heart of every Scotsman. Instead, the racecourse has been allowed to nibble away bits of the Links to suit its own purpose, with the result that the double running-rails now hinder play on most of the holes.

A dedicated writer on the history of the game, David Hamilton, begins a sentimental reference to Musselburgh Old Links in his *Good Golf Guide to Scotland* with the following information;

No telephone. Visitors freely admitted. A small green fee is sometimes collected if a local council official attends. There is no clubhouse, and the starting point is difficult to find.

The book was published in 1982 and there is now a bleak, single-storey windowless Clubhouse with a pool table and a bar, a storeroom-cum-changing bay, no shower and a couple of wash-hand basins. Otherwise it's just as David Hamilton wrote in 1982 and gives some idea of what awaits the coachloads of home and overseas visitors anxious to see what exists of the birthplace of world golf as known today.

How the Americans would love to pick it up, turf by turf, and lovingly re-create it, contours, bunkers and all, in one of their National Parks. Something like another Restoration-of-the-City-of Williamsburg project. Complete with full-size waxwork figures in traditional costumes scattered around the sward. Or better still, why not a Maxwell-Murdoch-Hanson-or-Rowlands-sponsored attempt to emulate what John D. Rockefeller did at Williamsburg, and take on the restoration of Musselburgh?

The great old Golf-houses could be restored with loving care and hired out for banquets and corporate functions; shop concessions could be offered on franchise for the sale of old hickory woods, guttie balls and similar artifacts of bygone golfing days; and books, maps and scorecards would be bought up *ad infinitum* by each coachload of starry-eyed afficionados.

The course side of Mrs Forman's celebrated pub beyond the third green could come alive again, at the back of which yesterday's golfers used to stop for a refreshing draught through a hole in the wall on their way round – rather as they still do about 5 miles from my home, at Whitewebbs Golf Club, Enfield, where course etiquette still includes a halt at the 14th for a drink bought from the back of the thousand-year-old 'King & Tinker', reputed to be the smallest pub in the county. Smallest or not, its beer sales are probably treble those at the surrounding temples of Bacchus, from what I can remember of the routine stoppage and crowd scene at the 14th when I last played there 30 years ago.

In June 1989, members of the British Golf Collectors Society, clad in the traditional period golfing costume and carrying pre-1928 hickory-shafted clubs, assembled at

Musselburgh Old Links for the Scottish Hickory Championships. David Hamilton, a founder member, wrote in the autumn issue of the Society magazine on the lighter side of the event, but in keeping with my earlier quotation from his 1982 book, he had much to say about degeneration of the Links.

As an eminent West of Scotland surgeon and devotee of the historic background to the game, his comments and frustration on the decline of Musselburgh come through as incisively, no doubt, as his scalpel strokes. I quote:

Musselburgh links are surviving, but only just. The owners are the District Council and little money is given for upkeep. The interests of the race meetings come first, and major earthworks are destroying the course even further. The Musselburgh Old Course Club is doing its best to protect what remains of the original course, putting in their own money, and the greens are increasingly good while some of the old bunkers are being found and revived.

Certainly it is all very pleasant to be able to turn up and play at the birthplace of the modern game without fee or formality, despite having to fight your way through the fences of a racecourse among local youths pressing from all sides. But there comes a point when we must ask whether this is genuine benign neglect and not another example of Scottish inertia in the face of obvious need.

It cannot be said that Musselburgh must decay because there are too many golf courses in Scotland, as the waiting lists to join them are full and lengthy. It cannot be said there are no golfing visitors, since the Scottish east coast clubs to north and south of Musselburgh are inundated with busloads of golfing visitors. Nor can it be said that Scotland has done so much for the history of golf already that nothing else need be done; almost nothing has been done.

Any nation with flair and pride would many years ago have made Musselburgh a place of homage. Not necessarily covered the hallowed nine holes with a dome; not necessarily provided a museum and rental of hickories and re-made gutties for play; not necessarily refurbished the ancient clubhouses; the minimum that could have been done would be to restore the ancient layout, renovate the old bunkers, and provide a thoughtful scorecard and map of the town, marking the sites of historical golfing interest.

And could we not let a Mrs Forman serve refreshments again through the hatch? The answer is that the Licensing Acts (Scotland) prohibit serving of drink in pubs for consumption in the open air. If Mrs Forman's was allowed to serve in this way who knows, say the puritans, what other devilish practices might follow!

Does Scotland really deserve the Old Links at Musselburgh?

That same Golf Collectors Society again held its Scottish Hickory Club Championship on the old Musselburgh Links on 1 June 1990 and this time Sam Morley was one of the 54 competitors.

At Mrs Forman's, the 200-year-old tavern adjacent to the third hole and often featured in the history books – but now in 20th century corporate-brewery 'livery' of pristine whitewash, illuminated lager adverts, and a 'parasol' of modern pan-tiles – we met up for an excellent buffet lunch, washed down in my case by a pint of Tennants draught. The cluttered boxroom in the little Clubhouse that did duty as a changing room was gallantly surrendered to the half-dozen

Mrs Forman's c1840
(Low-level boards on side wall cover old 'take-away servery'!)

Mrs Forman's 1990
Two originals by Adam Latto, Musselburgh. *(Well, he copied the upper from an original!)*

or so members' wives among us, while we hardy males did the best we could in and around our cars parked in front of the racecourse grandstand. My five borrowed left-handed hickories were all just a little bit older than me and kindly loaned by David White. He brought along no fewer than 12 sets of clubs from his Seaford collection for his friends, and each of us was handed his advisory sheet worded as follows;

A FEW NOTES ABOUT HICKORY CLUBS

The clubs you will play with today are ancient. None are less than 60 years old and one or two are approaching their centenary. All have been carefully prepared for today's event – shafts cleaned & treated with linseed oil and grips replaced or repaired. Treat them with respect and don't expect too much from them. Certainly don't expect them to perform like modern clubs of today.

You will have the following clubs;
1)	Driver or Brassie (No 1 or 2 wood) good for 180–190yds.
2)	Driving Iron (a mixture, about 2/3/4 iron) good for 155/175 yds.
3)	Mashie (angle of about a 5 iron) good for about 140/150 yds.
4)	Mashie Niblick (angle of about an 8½ iron) good for 120 and less.
5)	Putter.

The secret: S W I N G   S L O W L Y

Do not crunch the ball by taking a divot, as this will:

a) break the club,
b) hurt your hands,
c) break my heart.

A smooth, sweeping stroke is the only one that will work with these old weapons and remember, the secret is to SWING SLOWLY.

THE BALL

The modern ball of lower compression (preferably of wound design) will respond better with these clubs. A 100 compression ball is useless, 90 is better and a ladies 80 compression best.

To replace a broken hickory shaft is more expensive than replacing a modern Aldila Boron shaft so PLEASE . . . .*swing slowly and smoothly*, no crunching divots, be patient. SWING SLOWLY !!!!!!!!!!

Well, I swung slowly – when I remembered – and didn't break a club. Didn't break a hundred either, playing twice round the old nine-hole course, most of it in the rain and with waterproofs and umbrella keeping nice and dry in the boot of the car.

By overnighting there and asking around, much of what was gleaned from other opinions for the earlier part of this chapter can now be supplemented.

Musselburgh Links are leased from East Lothian District Council by the Musselburgh Joint Racing Committee, consisting of members of Ayr Racecourse Ltd and East Lothian District Council. The Council thereby being both landlord and tenant. The Golf Links are run by the District Council with Peter Cunnningham as its paid Manager. He is also Starter, in his fifth year as Captain of the Old Course Golf Club, Manager of the Clubhouse, Barman, and also

Chef when 'visiting firemen' book a meal in advance. He also helps a greenkeeping staff of one to look after the course. He is constantly at odds with the District Council as he badgers them to improve the course image and facilities for visitors – although he also has the Hamburger-stand concession in the public enclosure on their race days. In this instance there was to be a race meeting the day after our visit.

Flat-racing has taken place at Musselburgh Links since 1816 on a track shared with a nine-hole golf course, but in 1985 National Hunt racing was introduced. This meant enlarging the circuit and introducing a second and parallel running rail which repeatedly cuts across the line of play. Balls coming to rest in the 90-feet ribbon of turf between the two sets of rails have to be played, if found, out of 4–6 inches of lush grass instead of 'creamed-off' close-mown fairways.

And whereas in those halcyon days of yore the horses ran round flagged stakes stuck in the ground at 10-yard intervals on the morning of race days – as they still do at our local point-to-point and at many race-tracks visited all over the world in the past 30 years (yes, I'm a racing enthusiast too) – here at Musselburgh were double lines of 4 inch diameter white tubes, 90 feet apart, over or under – and often against – which a golfer would hit his ball several times on the way round.

The 'horsey' Council gave the golfers the little wooden Clubhouse as a 'bag of sweets' in compensation for riding roughshod (metaphorically) over their playground, and the Musselburgh Links Preservation Society took the case up before the Ombudsman about six years ago – but claimed that the vested interests of gambling won the day. It meant desecration of a 200-year-old golfing shrine that attracts tens of thousands of 'worshippers' throughout the year for the sake of those who came to work, watch or wager on Musselburgh's 12 days of Flat and 8 days of National Hunt racing over the same period. Most of whom would benefit if better facilities were provided for them elsewhere.

With all the land available within a 25-miles radius of Edinburgh, it's hard to understand why the city's only racecourse has to cannibalise an historic monument for its own voracious appetite.

But apathy is there for all to see. Here we have a busy historic town on the old A1, now the A199, 7 miles from Edinburgh, with a population of about 18,000, but without a proper bookshop. Only an antiquarian bookseller, specialising in golf memorabilia, and trading from a converted lock-up garage in a residential riverside back street about a drive and a wedge from either the Links or the High Street shops. Adam Latto is a founder member of the Links Preservation Society and well worth a visit at Latto Books, 3 Eskside East, Musselburgh, EH21 7RU.

Personally, I think the old Musselburgh Links will never rise from its ashes (more metaphoricals!) until the racing fraternity is catered for elsewhere; a Links Management Committee is formed to administer it (as at other public courses like St Andrews or Carnoustie); and a self-respecting visitors' bureau is created with modern catering, changing, and souvenir shopping facilities for those tens of thousands who come from all parts of the globe to pay homage – and who go away wondering if they've come to the right place! And until there is a decent hotel or two in the area offering facilities a little more upmarket than the one in which I stayed, which had eight bedrooms served by one communal bathroom-cum-lavatory!

Everybody spoke of land reclaimed from the Forth several years ago on which an 18-hole course is to be built, but nobody knows when. The local authority claims it hasn't the money to develop it. Then why don't they let the racing folk develop it? They could certainly do with something more in keeping with the excellent racecourse facilities at Ayr on the other coast instead of their own uninspiring set-up at Musselburgh. The world of entrepreneurial Golf would then gladly raise funds for bringing the game's oldest original course and its features into the twenty-first century, while ensuring it would lose none of its old image in so doing.

Over to you now, you big-spending corporate benefactors, get your cheque-books out and earn yourselves a spot in the Golfing Halls of Fame. Maybe even a Scottish peerage.

But will the East Lothian District Council ever relinquish its stranglehold on the patient and allow a kiss of life from others?

4

Royal Burgess

The drive to and through Edinburgh to Royal Burgess Golf Club, on the western perimeter of the City, was trouble-free, largely as a result of taking the route recommended by Gordon Vanreenen, Secretary of Muirfield. He said to ignore the road signs pointing to 'Forth Road Bridge – avoiding the City Centre', and keep right on into town and out the other end. I did just that and was pleasantly surprised how easy it was to get through. Traffic turned out to be about a quarter of what could be expected in the centre of London at 2.30 on a Monday afternoon.

I was now en route to the first meeting of my pre-arranged programme. Everything so far had been a bonus thanks to a life-long tendency to 'stop and smell the flowers'.

Ian Hume, Secretary of the Scottish Golf Union, had applied for a copy of *If it wasn't for Golf . . . !* prior to publication, and had subsequently arranged for it to be reviewed in *Scottish Golfer*, the monthly magazine of SGU. I was now on my way to discuss how best the book could be further marketed.

When asked on the phone the best way of getting to his office from the centre of Edinburgh, he'd said to come out of the City on the route marked 'Forth Road Bridge' and that Royal Burgess Golf Club would be on the right when I reached the suburb of Barnton. He and his staff would be found in offices that were once the greenkeeper's house, and there might well be a pot of tea at the ready.

Everything came out as he said. The ex-greenkeepers house proved to be an attractive two-storey building close to the entrance to the course and car park, the tea was hot, fresh and strong, and a plateful of crisp 'bikkies' completed the 'natives-are-friendly' message. We spent nearly an hour with hardly a word on the original purpose of the visit: there was so much to learn on the history of my surroundings.

It is amazing to think that until this venture I'd never even heard of the Royal Burgess Golf Club, yet it claimed to be the oldest Golf Club in the world! (I can almost hear the cry, 'Not another one?').

Well, the Royal Burgess Golfing Society of Edinburgh claims 1735 as its foundation date and it celebrated its 250th birthday in July 1985. (But Henderson and Stirk in *Royal Blackheath* dispute this and put the origin of the Society around 1770). The 'Royal' prefix was acquired when King George V granted patronage in 1929.

The Prince of Wales (later to be Edward VIII, and later still Duke of Windsor) accepted Captaincy of the Club on its 200th anniversary in 1935 and presented a gold ball, instead of the customary silver one, to be hung on the traditional Silver Club. He'd been a keen golfer since his schooldays and had earlier accepted Captaincy of the Royal and Ancient Golf Club of St Andrews in 1922. He confided once that his father, King George V, had also been an addict, but decided to give it up as he didn't think it was right for one who ruled over an Empire on which the sun was said never to set, to be seen or heard venting spleen when trying to hit a little ball with a bent stick!

The name 'Burgess' stems from 'burghers', or property-owning citizens. The Burgess Golfing Society of Edinburgh

"…Or in the words of my Lords Spiritual and Temporal … ** !!x!! !"

started its long and colourful history playing golf on Bruntsfield Links, situated on the southern side of the City about half a mile from the Castle. Comprising six holes, it was too far inland from the Forth Estuary to be considered as links in the true meaning of the word. Being common ground Edinburgh citizenry had free use of the course, as in fact have those who play there today. The masonic beginnings of the Burgess Golfing Society are as shrouded in mystery as those of the Hon. Company, so much so that no records exist prior to the first recorded minutes of April 1773.

A Bruntsfield Links Golfing Society came into being during this period, as a spin-off from 'The Burgess', after differences of opinion between some of the members. Stories vary as to just how and what they differed over, but the popular belief is that it was political. This was not very long after the 1745 Jacobite rebellion when passions ran high. The drinking of loyal toasts to the Crown at Scottish dinners didn't come easy to those whose friends and relations had died in battle or on the gallows for supporting Bonnie Prince Charlie.

(Their dinners must have been almost as lively as some of the AGM's held in recent times at my own club!)

But the two Societies continued to share Bruntsfield links for the next hundred years or more, until its crowded and deteriorating conditions had them joining the action out at Musselburgh, where they each built their own Golf-house in the 1870s.

And now almost another hundred years have passed since 1895, when the Burgess had their own course built out at Barnton on 100 acres of land leased at £1400 a year. They then bought the freeholders out in stages, acquiring the last piece in 1977.

Taken on a conducted tour of the magnificent Clubhouse, with its priceless memorabilia and trophies, I was impressed

by the 120-year-old link with its old base in the shape of the
'Rhind Stone'. In the previous chapter I referred to the
Burgess's abandoned Golf-house as being one of those
without any signs of identity. The Club was so proud of its
'Rhind Stone' – a bas-relief panel carved in stone by John
Rhind, ARSA, an Edinburgh sculptor, and set into the Golf-
house frontage when it was built in 1875 – that they hacked
it out of the Musselburgh building and transferred it to their
new home when moving to Barnton in 1895. It was admired
and prized by all who used the Links and when carted away
some of the older caddies followed it to the outskirts of
Edinburgh, as they would a hearse carrying an old friend to
his burial. For the last 95 years it has graced the outside wall
facing the 18th green at Barnton and is shown here depicting a
scene at the Club's original home, Bruntsfield Links, with
two members – identified as friends of the artist – and their
caddies, with Edinburgh Castle in the background.

The Chronicle of the Royal Burgess Golfing Society, vol. 1, by J.
Cameron Robbie, was published in 1937. It covers the
Club's first 200 years. From it more was learned of that first
Silver Club Competition on Leith Links.

Much has been written over the years of the part played
by the Hon. Golfers in drawing up the first Rules of Golf for
the purpose of that event but very little – to my knowledge –
on how it was to be organised. George Pottinger refers to
such Regulations but provides little detail, although he
reproduces the famous original Rules of Play in full, and a
copy of which hangs on the Clubhouse wall at Muirfield.

Yet J. Cameron Robbie thought those Competition
Regulations sufficiently important and interesting to
reproduce them in full in Appendix IV of his Burgess book,
headed, 'INFORMATION from MINUTE BOOKS etc of the TOWN
COUNCIL of EDINBURGH relating to Golfing Matters in general

The Rhind Stone

and to the BURGESS GOLFING SOCIETY in particular, 1554–1894'. As he says in his footnote: 'These Regulations of 1744 might well be considered the 'Magna Carta' for open competition in Golf.'

That being the case they are well worth re-presentation here exactly as taken from the Edinburgh Town Council's minute book entry of that date:

7th March 1744. Copy Regulations of Play for the Silver Club given, for open competition, by the Magistrates of Edinburgh in 1744, and now in the custody of The Honourable Company of Edinburgh Golfers at Muirfield. (Vol.1 xiv. p. 207.)

It being represented in Council that several gentlemen of Honour, Skilful in the ancient and healthfull exercise of the Golf, had from time to time applied to seaverall of the members of the [Town] Council for a Silver Club to be annually played for on the Links of Leith, at such time, and upon such conditions as the Magistrates and Council should think proper; and it being reported that the gentlemen golfers had drawn up a scroll, at the desire of Magistratts, of such articles and conditions as to them seemed most expedient as proper Regulations to be observed by the gentlemen who should yearly offer to play for the said Silver Club which were produced and read in Councill the tenor whereof follows:

1.   As many Noblemen or gentlemen or other golfers from any part of Great Britain or Ireland as shall book themselves eight days before, or upon any of the lawfull days of the week immediately preceeding the day appointed by the Magistrates and Councill for the Annual Match, shall have the priveledge of playing for the said Club, each

signer paying five shillings sterling at signing in a book to be provided for that purpose, which is to ly in Mrs. Clephen's House in Leith, or such other house as afterwards the subscribers shall appoint from year to year; and the Regulations approved of by the Magistrates and Councill shall be recorded at the beginning of said book.

2. On the morning before playing small bits of paper marked with the figures 1, 2, 3, &c. according to the number of players shall be put into a bonnet, and drawn by the signers, and every couple shall be matched according to the figures by them drawn, beginning with number 1, 2, and so on; but if there shall be a great number of subscribers they shall be matched in threes; and after the parties are thus matched, in case there be an odd number, the gentleman who draws it shall play along with the last set.

3. After the figures are drawn, the set or match beginning with No. 1, &c., shall go out first with a clerk to mark down every stroke each of them shall take to every hole, then, by the time they are at the Sawmill Hole, the second set, beginning with Nos. 3 & 4 according as the match shall be made shall strike off; and so all the rest in the same order, each set haveing a clerk; and when the match is ended, a scrutiny of the whole clerks books or jottings is to be made, and the player who shall appear to have won the greatest number of Holes shall be declared to be the winner of the match; And if there shall be two, three, or more that are equal then these two or three, &c., must play a round themselves in the order of their figures, before they go off the ground, to determine the match.

4.   The Crowns given in are solely to be at the disposall of the victor.

5.   Every victor is to append a gold or silver peice as he pleases, to the Club, for the year he wins.

6.   That every victor shall, at the receiving the Club, give sufficient caution to the Magistrates and Councill of Edinburgh for Fifty pounds Sterling for delivering back the Club to their hands one month before it is to be played for again.

7.   That the Club is declared to be allways the Property of the Good Town.

8.   That if any dispute shall happen betwixt any of the parties the same shall be determined by the other subscribers not concerned in the debate.

9.   That the victor shall be called *Captain of the Golf*, and all disputes touching the Golf amongst Golfers shall be determined by the Captain, and any two or three of the subscribers he shall call to his assistance, and that the Captain shall be intitled next year to the first ticket without drawing.

10. That no coaches, chaises, or other wheel machines, or people on horse back, are to be allowed to go through the Links, but by the high roads, when the match for the Silver club is a playing, or at any other time, and that the said Captain shall from year to year have the care and inspection of the Links, and shall be at liberty to complain to the Lord Provost and Magistrates of any encroachments made upon them by high roads or otherwise.

11. The subscribers shall have power, if the day appointed for the match shall be improper for playing it, to adjourn to another day, upon which it is fit for playing, the match shall proceed.

Lastly. It is declared that upon no pretence whatsoever the City of Edinburgh shall be put to any sort of expence upon account of playing for the said Club annually, except to intimate by Tuck of Drum, through the City the day upon which it shall be annually played for, such time before the match as the Magistrates and Council shall think proper, and to send the Silver Club to Leith upon the morning appointed for the match.

Which Regulations having been considered by the Magistrates and Council, they with the extraordinary Deacons, approved thereof with and under this express condition that nothing contained in the above Regulations shall in any sort prejudge the Magistracy and Council to dispose in few or otherwise of all or any part of the Links of Leith as they shall think proper, and they hereby authorise the Treasurer to cause make a Silver club not exceeding the value of Fifteen pounds sterling to be played for annually upon the above conditions: With power to the Captain of the Golf, and any two of the subscribers to make such orders for regulating the manner of playing from time to time as they shall think proper, and do hereby appoint the first Munday of Aprile yearly as the day for playing the Annual Match for the Silver Club.

(Signed) JOHN COUTTS, PROVOST.

It came as quite a surprise to learn that the famous Silver Club competition was decided on Match – not Stroke – play, and that the Regulations were laid down by the Town Council – not by the Hon. Golfers as so many are led to believe; though they probably helped the boys up at the Town Hall in the framing of the Golfing MAGNA CARTA – just 529 years after King John signed that other one!

As for reaching a decision on the real age of the Burgess, Henderson and Stirk's argument in *Royal Blackheath* is difficult to override. Despite exhaustive research they could find nothing to point to the existence of a Burgess Society earlier than the first minutes of 1773.

Of course, many of the early members must have knocked around on the Bruntsfield links for years before their Society was formed, and it's my belief that in their anxiety to outstrip their rivals for the title of oldest, one or two eager beavers might have added the number of years they'd been wielding their hickory shafted clubs out at Bruntsfield to the age of their newly-formed Society.

The same applies to Bruntsfield Links Golf Club which claims 1761 as its formation date, but whose first minute book starts in 1787.

But they are all without doubt worthy of deference even if they might happen to be slightly younger than claimed.

It is also a little confusing the way history books switch from 'Society' to 'Club' when referring to these early Scottish groups. Even back in 1875 Clark's *Golf* writes of Bruntsfield Links Golf Club: 'The first minute book in the possession of the Club dates from 1787, in which year the Club underwent conversion from a Society to a Club, whatever that may mean!' In today's golfing circles it is generally understood that a Club will have its own premises, although facilities provided for its members may or may not include a private course to play on. A Society would have neither premises nor golf-course, and would draw its members from golfing enthusiasts among a larger group involved in other activities.

This subject is enlarged upon in chapter 5 of *If it wasn't for Golf . . . !*, and as it includes the story of how The Honourable Company of Edinburgh Golfers spawned the Horrible Company of Cambridge Golfers it's worth repeating here for those unfortunates who missed it first time round. To avoid boring those who didn't I suggest they skip the next few pages and move on to Chapter 5.

A Golfing Society is a 'closed-shop' of dedicated golf addicts. It usually begins when people sharing a common interest – be it to work, play, teach, learn, cure, protect or amuse – form an inner circle among those of its number familiar with the game.

So just as the House of Commons, as does the House of Lords, have its own Golfing Society among those who make our laws, so does each of the Police Divisions that enforce them, and the Barristers and Judges who interpret them. Not to mention the Prison Officers guarding those who break 'em.

They can be found as frequently among Freemasons, Rotarians, Buffaloes, Trade Associations, Chambers of Commerce, Airlines, Town Halls, H.M. Forces, Hospitals, Colleges, Polytechnics and Old Boys Associations, as among British Airways, Gas, Oil, Telecom, Electricity, Water, Rail . . .

Devotees of the game among Writers, Publishers and Journalists generally form themselves into Societies, as do Jockeys, Stage Performers and Income Tax Inspectors. Many of the noble Clubs around Pall Mall boast one among their members as do more plebeian establishments elsewhere.

Doctors, Dentists, Architects, Lawyers, Engineers, Publicans, Broadcasters, Surveyors, and Lord-knows how many more brainy and brawny groups have their local and national Golfing Societies. There's a left-handed Society in most civilised countries, as there is among one-armed, one-legged, and no doubt one-eyed enthusiasts for the game. Most Golf Clubs have their own inner 'closed shops' – made up from those of its members that choose to form a Society because they share a common experience, activity or peculiarity. Hence the Over-forties; Over-sixties; Past-Captains; Hole-in-one; ex-Army -Navy or -R.A.F. Golfing Societies . . . . Whether they meet weekly, monthly, quarterly, or annually, all Golfing Societies have one thing in common. A pre-arranged plan to take time off from the daily round and get together at a chosen golf course other than the one they normally play at weekends. It could be in the next parish, village, town, county, country or continent.

The day, or days, away with a good Society is usually made up of competitive golf, prize-giving, sweepstakes for golf balls, possibly too much food, certainly too much drink, and nowhere near enough sleep. At least, with most of the folks I've been away with . . . .

Where Societies have a number of meetings in a year, one or more can be declared a guest day; whereby each member brings along a pal. Often the same pal each time. I suppose Reg Davies was my guest at Eccentric Club Golfing Society meetings about as often as I was his at those of the British Dental Association Golfing Society. It has been said we each knew more among the other's Society than did many of its own less-gregarious followers. As a result his 'trophy-room' shelves are stacked with about as many Eccentric cut-glass drinking goblets as mine are with silver tankards engraved BDAGS.

It was as his guest after golf, prize-giving, ball-sweep and speeches at Thorndon Park Golf Club one year that I sat down to dinner across from Millice Freeman – a dental officer with the Ministry of Health. His plain blue silk tie with a single large golfing motif had me asking the meaning of the initials HCCG woven into it. 'Horrible Company of Cambridge Golfers' he replied, and with little further prompting told the story behind it.

When he was a young man at Cambridge, and a member of its famous Gog and Magog Golf Club, he decided – together with three equally-addicted, low-handicap pals – on a golfing holiday in Scotland, playing some of its great courses – including Muirfield, home of the Honourable Company of Edinburgh Golfers; where they duly presented themselves at the Secretary's office and asked permission to pay a green fee and play a round. A fellow-member at Gog and Magog was also a member at Muirfield, and had assured them that if they just mentioned his name to the Secretary the doors would be flung open wide by way of a welcome. Well, they mentioned his name good and loud, but the doors remained bolted and barred. In vain they told of their prowess at the game and awareness of the behaviour and etiquette expected of them, but the man in charge was adamant. Without a letter of introduction from their own Club Secretary, or from the friend and member to whom they referred, they could not enter the illustrious home of the Honourable Company of Edinburgh Golfers, and were barred from placing mortal feet on its sacred fairways.

They pleaded how far they'd travelled just to walk on the hallowed turf, and took an oath that should any of it be disturbed by their efforts it would be carefully re-instated, right way up, before attempting another shot. For all the effect it had they might just as well have pleaded with the grey stone blocks of which the clubhouse was built. The door remained firmly closed.

Turning away in despair one of the four said bitterly, 'It's not fair, when you think of the number of Scots who come sightseeing around historic old Cambridge, and are allowed to play golf on our historic old "Gogs" without ever being asked to produce credentials. We wouldn't dream of being discourteous to folks who'd come all that way to enjoy our treasured heritage.' Or words to that effect.

This must have found a chink in the old curmudgeon's armour because he relented sufficiently to growl, still with some reluctance, 'All right , I'll let you play a round of golf but you're not allowed to use the Clubhouse'. To which the boys replied with genuine delight, 'That's very kind, Sir, and thank you very much. But surely you'll let us use the locker rooms to change our clothes?' 'No', was the firm response. 'The Clubhouse and locker rooms are for members and their guests only. You'll have to make do as best you can in the trolley-shed or in your own motor-car.' And that was final.

Well, they made do as best they could in the trolley-shed and motor-car. Once having played, they went in search of a pub or hotel to rinse the dust from parched East Anglian throats. While doing so they mulled over the cavalier treatment meted out by the Honourable Company of Edinburgh Golfers – and decided to commemorate the experience by forming the 'Horrible Company of Cambridgeshire Golfers'!

They would meet each year at Muirfield on the anniversary of the first visit and play a Stableford competition – making sure to take along the vital written credentials with them. They would book into the adjoining Greywalls Hotel, where the quality of food, wine and service would serve as a reminder of the Muirfield catering standards denied them on the day. After dinner there would be prize-giving, toasts and speeches, followed by the Annual General Meeting of the HCCG. A Captain, Vice-Captain, Secretary, and Treasurer would be elected.

Well, not exactly elected, because with but four positions to fill from a full membership of four, the honours would be passed around in rotation. The new Captain would call for a magnum of champagne to celebrate his appointment and to launch the Society on yet another successful year.

A special tie was designed, to be worn at all meetings of the Society, and as frequently as possible when in the company of other golfers, so that it could be explained to those curious enough to ask its origin.

And this ritual they continued to follow for the next thirty years or more.

Well, there we have a blow-by-blow account of how the very first Golfing Society in the land unwittingly spawned a new one on or around its 200th birthday.

Unlike its illustrious ancestor, the new Society will not be making the history books. Other than this one, of course. Never having recruited new members it will hang up its hat when the last of its four founders has done likewise. A pity, really, because the HCCG by this time might well have qualified for its own ceremonial Silver Club and Balls.

5

St Andrews – 1

Repainting the 100-year-old Forth Bridge is a colloquial way of defining a never-ending task; no sooner has the maintenance team slapped the last brushful on at the far end, so it's said, then it's time to go back and start all over again.

Leaving 'The Burgess' and joining streams of commuters heading westwards from the City for about 8 miles to the Forth Road Bridge (toll 40p) and crossing into Fife, I looked in vain for painters clinging to the majestic spans of the Rail Bridge about a quarter of a mile upstream, but they were nowhere to be seen. Whether it meant they were all working on the under- or perhaps far-side, or that British Rail now had a spray-on, anti-corrosive treatment that needed application only once every ten years, or just that the boys happened to be on their tea-break at that particular moment, I did not find out until almost a year later.

On 3 March 1990 the Forth Rail Bridge was exactly 100 years old. Thanks to the research and subsequent write-up by the *Sunday Telegraph* of that date, much was learned statistically that was not known hitherto . Not by me, that is. For instance:

1.   The bridge incorporates the first example of cantilever building, whereby two spans of 1700

feet each were achieved, against the hitherto world record of a 495-foot span over the Niagara Falls.

2. It was hailed as the eighth wonder of the world on completion, and Heads of State from both the civilised and not-unduly-so countries throughout the world came to marvel at its grandeur and imaginative proportions.

3. It took seven years to complete and, with frequent gales, an average of 22 days' work a month was difficult to maintain. Four rowing boats, each with a crew of two, were always in the water below the working areas. During those seven years they saved eight lives and recovered 8,000 caps blown off the heads of those working above.

4. Even though I failed to spot them when crossing on the Road Bridge, there is a permanent maintenance staff of 28 painters, 7 riggers, 5 railway track fitters, and 2 rescue boatmen. The latter are never off the water when the others are on the job as, with no vertical parts to the structure and the only horizontal one being the permanent way, danger lurks at all times.

5. Its renowned never-ending maintenance programme underwrites the safety of 200 trains a day passing over it, but safety was built-in with the Victorian standards of its design. It took 56,000 tons of steel to cater for those two 1,700-foot spans, whereas it took but 39,000 tons to build its 'young brother', the Forth Road Bridge, with its single span of 3,300 feet.

The 25-year-old, 2 mile-long Road Bridge was just as impressive a structure. Whether there is another team of painters clambering around for life over its steel tracery is something British Rail were unable to say when I phoned their PR office.

Sight of the old Rail Bridge brought back more memories of my old RN days, spanning the river as it did a few hundred yards downstream of the entrance into Rosyth Dockyard. With one or two notable exceptions any ship in the Home Fleet could steam under it, subject to tides, but one of the standard questions on seamanship, when it came to being tested for possible promotion, was how to go about striking topmast if one were in charge of the working party on HMS *Hood* or *Repulse* when about to sail under the Forth Bridge. Never mind that the topmost tip of the mainmast on a 1200-ton V and W destroyer (my ship at the time was HMS *Verdun*) was not as high above the water-line as the foc'stle deck of one of those battle-wagons – to the best of my memory, that is.

I must say that, although knowing as much then about that mind-boggling evolution as my grand-daughter does today, the outcome was that I passed with flying colours. Well, passed anyway. The bloke asking the questions must have known even less than I did and, thinking back, between us we could easily have dismasted the Home Fleet. The hard way!

Still with the Navy, my next appointment was at Limekilns, near Rosyth, with a weapons-control officer at his home. The son of a fellow-member of my Golf Club, he'd just about reached the end of 21 years service and his dad had suggested he might be able to help with some of the research needed for that Naval book I'll probably still be trying to write ten years hence.

Once again my arrival coincided with the kettle boiling, and over a pot of tea we talked of ships, string, sealing wax, service life in general, and my project in particular, until it was time for him to point me in the right direction for the final lap of an epic first day's run of almost 500 miles.

During 20-plus years as editor of the *Sunday Express*, Sir John Junor would often write a pithy double column on the leader page, airing his views on the passing show, especially on some of the more sordid and unsavoury examples of Sodom and Gomorrah life-styles in our cities today. To make a telling point he would compare them to the homespun, God-fearing paths of moral rectitude trodden by those who lived out their lives far from the madding crowd in his home town of Auchtermuchty. Many's the Sunday morning he's had me spluttering over the cornflakes while my wife read out his latest journalistic gem. And now, speeding through Auchtermuchty High Street, half way between Rosyth and St Andrews, I wondered if all was in fact as John Junor believed it to be behind those dark granite walls and multi-paned first-floor windows. Was it possible that his paragons of virtue were busy turning his town into another Peyton Place behind those lace curtains, even during the few moments it took to speed by in the evening sunshine? We'll never know, and probably it's best not to. Nothing very good ever comes from destroying a legend!

Then came journey's end: the 'Holy City' itself! Turning the last bend in the tortuous road leading into St Andrews, suddenly it was there to be seen for the very first time. The notorious 17th green – the Road Hole; the little stone hump-backed bridge over the fast-running Swilken Burn; and the 18th fairway stretching out towards the majestic HQ of the Royal and Ancient Golf Club of St Andrews in the distance. Only instead of cheering TV hordes packed tightly around the familiar playing areas, the wide expanse of four 18-hole golf courses – the Old, New, Jubilee, and Eden – was almost deserted.

St Andrews is steeped in history, and not just golfing history. Its University is the oldest in Scotland – some claim in Britain – and its Cathedral was the largest, until John Knox did his inflammatory 'Ian Paisley' stuff around 1560.

The Industrial Revolution completely revitalised the country between the mid eighteenth and nineteenth centuries. Before that, Scotland – and, in fact, Britain as a whole – was an agricultural nation 'contending with nature for subsistence', say the historians. Most continental countries were way ahead of us in art, science, mechanics, navigation, and engineering. Although an island race, we had no real navy and even had to buy the fish caught off our own shores from the Dutch. It was the Dutch, too, who bought the raw wool from the Scottish sheep farmers, which they processed, dyed, and sold back as finished manufactured goods – much the same as we did with American cotton 400 years later. And in the course of ferrying wool and herrings between the two countries, those Dutch seamen would step ashore for a game of 'Kolven' and, in so doing, planted its seed among the curious spectators.

It is now more than 500 years since those first golf 'seeds' were sown on the immortal St Andrews links. Anyone with a couple of clubs and a ball could amuse themselves knocking that ball about, and then holes came to be cut in the turf to give some purpose and direction to the knock.

At first there were 11 such holes, stretching from somewhere near the Castle out to the farthermost point on the Bay. Having reached this, players would then turn round and play their way back to town using the same holes. Thereby a round of golf at St Andrews in the early days would consist of 22 holes. With all that traffic, those 11 holes were subjected to a lot of wear; so larger putting areas were created and two holes cut in each – one being used for the journey out and the other for the trip back. Hence the famous double-greens of St Andrews.

One of the 13 original Rules of Golf said that after holing out a player should tee his ball up for the next hole no farther than two club lengths away from the one he'd just completed. Well, as this was all before the days of wooden and plastic pegs, the standard practice was to make a mini-mound with a little sand. The links consisting of a thin crust of turf on a natural sand base, the nearest available source of tee-building material was from the bottom of the hole just played. There were no steel linings to the holes in those days, with the result that what was a neat $4\frac{1}{2}''$ diameter hole soon became a not-so-neat 7" one; and so deep that it was impossible to retrieve a ball from the bottom. Eventually, and in order to prevent further broken finger nails and dislocated shoulders, the rules were modified and separate teeing grounds introduced in 1846.

Some time earlier the Council needed more land to enlarge the town. So they chopped out the first two holes on the Links and the last two back, and on the ground thus acquired built The Scores development and the buildings lining it, stretching back to the vicinity of the Castle.

That is how the 22-hole St Andrews Old Course became an 18-holer, and the model for countless thousands of golf courses built around the world thereafter. It also means that millions of addicts flogging their way round those thousands of courses every weekend, start their Sunday lunch about an hour earlier than they might otherwise have done had St Andrews stayed the way it was!

In 1974, the St Andrews Town Council was absorbed into the East Fife District Council but its golf courses were left to be administered by the St Andrews Links Trust and maintained by a Management Committee. The Royal and Ancient Golf Club of St Andrews has three representatives on the Trust and four on the Committee, but has no priority

" Nice game - care for a quick pint in the 23rd?"

or right-of-play on any of the courses (four 18-hole and one 9-hole) that make up the links. While there is little difficulty in getting on to four of them, everybody wants to play on the Old. With the result that from April to October only four-balls are allowed and starting times are balloted for, although R&A members are allowed to reserve times during August and September.

Before playing, all must register and pay their fees to the Official Starter. Ensconced in his glass-shrouded office overlooking the first tee he is no respecter of passing 'greats' and his word is law in the interpretation of the St Andrews rules of play.

There's the story of Tom Weiskopf, who came over from the States to win the Open at Troon back in 1973, deciding to make a trip across country for a round on the Old at St Andrews before taking his trophy back home. Presenting himself at the Starter's Office, he requested permission to play and was asked for a 'twa poon' green fee [*it's currently 'twa-an'-twenty'!*]. He fished the money from his pocket and on receiving his ticket made his way to the competition tee and took a couple of loosening-up swings.

The Starter called to him from the window, 'Ye'll no' be playing off the back tees the day!'

'Sorry!' Tom called back politely, and went forward to the tee-of-the-day. Having cracked away a terrific drive he decided to try another for the fun of it. He took a second ball from his pocket and placed it on the peg.

Came the voice from the window. 'Ye'll no' be playing twa balls from the tee the day!'

With another 'Sorry!' Tom walked off down the fairway after his first ball and carried on round the course. At the 18th he was met by a most embarrassed R&A Secretary who, besides apologising for not being around to greet his distinguished visitor on arrival and take care of the formalities, produced two pounds from his own pocket and asked Tom for his ticket so that the matter could be cleared up with the Starter.

'No way,' laughed Tom, 'with this morning's experience that ole tickets's now a more treasured possession than the Cup I won yesterday!'

The Royal and Ancient Golf Club of St Andrews, with its unbroken series of Minutes going back to 1754 is, without doubt, the oldest Golf Club in the world. There is also no doubt that its initial membership was drawn from Freemasons pursuing the 'Healthfull exercise of the Golf', similar to those doing so in Edinburgh and as described in the earlier chapters. The St Andrews records show that they agreed to meet fortnightly at 11 am and play a round of the Links 'in accordance with the Rules of the annual Silver Club competition; subsequently to dine at Bailee Glass's and each to pay a shilling for his dinner. The absent as well as the present.'

The Rules were practically the same as those formulated by the Hon. Golfers of Edinburgh for the Open Silver Club competition at Leith links in1744, but the Silver Club at St Andrews was one subscribed for by its members. The Lord Provost of St Andrews was obviously not quite as bountiful as his opposite number on the other side of the Forth. But many of the top names in the golfing world of those times were common to both places.

The ubiquitous William St Clair of Roslin, Grand Master of Scottish Grand Lodge, was Captain of St Andrews in 1764, 1766, and 1768, and Captain of the Hon. Golfers in 1761, 1766, 1770 and 1771. (What with his three times Captaincy of St Andrews, four times of the Hon. Golfers, ten years' Presidency of the Hon. Company of Edinburgh Archers – besides his Masonic duties – he couldn't have spent much time back in Roslin). Another was Alexander Duncan, who is recorded as Captain of St Andrews in 1756, 1761, and 1781; of Blackheath in 1766 and 1767; and of the Hon. Golfers in 1781.

Captaincy in those days was not a transient honour passed in turn to deserving members of a Club. It was an honour, of course, but competed for and won by the player returning the best score in the annual Silver Club competition. That's how William St Clair came to be 'Captain of the Golf' both at St Andrews and the Hon. Golfers in the same year –1766 – and Alexander Duncan at the same two clubs in 1781. Like today's 'pot-hunters', they were probably forever playing and practising to have come out top so often. That's when they weren't travelling. With no Forth Bridge, motorways or airlines, it must have taken two or three days by land or sea between Edinburgh and St Andrews, and something like a week to London for the annual competition on Blackheath. Time and expense that only privileged folk could afford.

Although other Clubs and Societies came into being during the eighteenth century, rank, breeding or wealth were the prerequisites for acceptance into St Andrews, the Hon. Golfers, or Blackheath. Prerequisites, for there was still the 'black ball' procedure when candidates were interviewed. As already noted, many belonged to two of the foregoing Clubs, and some – like Alexander Duncan – to all three; but none of the names listed in their early membership records is to be found among the Burgess, Bruntsfield, or Musselburgh lists, which implies that membership of the last three was drawn from less exalted levels of society.

The records of the R&A show that 'on the 14th May 1754, 22 noblemen and gentlemen of Fife' formed themselves into 'The Society of St Andrews Golfers'. That same year they subscribed for the Silver Club, and William Landale,

'Merchant of St Andrews', won the competition; was declared 'Captain of the Golf'; and hung the first Silver Ball, with his name inscribed on it, from the Silver Club. The Rules were changed in 1824, when it was decided that Captaincy would be an honour attained with personality instead of a prize awarded for prowess.

The R&A was still a Society, without premises, and sharing a public course with the *hoi polloi* when, in 1834, King William IV became its patron and bestowed upon it the impressive title of 'The Royal and Ancient Golf Club of St Andrews'. A year later the newly established Club had negotiated to share premises with the older Union Club. It is said that silverware marked 'Union Club' is still used in the R&A dining room.

Academically, there is a slight uncertainty about the exact age of its 150-year-old clubhouse. Everard's *History of the Royal and Ancient Golf Club* tells how a Mr John Whyte-Melville laid the foundation stone in 1853 'with masonic honours'; while in J.R. Salmond's *The Story of the R&A* Major Belshes laid the foundation stone on 'Whitsunday 1854' with 'full masonic honours'. Irrespective of which is correct, it was near enough 100 years after William St Clair did his stuff for the Hon. Golfers at Leith in his capacity as Grand Master of Scottish Grand Lodge. It also tells us that Masonry still played a big part behind the scenes of Golf.

Besides its function as the ruling body on the game, the R&A is still a private members' club, with a current membership of 1,800; 1,050 from Great Britain and Ireland, and 750 scattered around the globe. Membership is an honour not lightly acquired, and is usually bestowed as a mark of esteem on those who have served the game well in this country or their own.

Although the four courses on the Links are the only 18-hole golf courses in St Andrews, the Royal and Ancient is by no means the only Golf Club in the town.

The New Golf Club was formed in 1902 and has its own Clubhouse on Gibson Place, a few yards from the 18th fairway of the Old Course. At the last count there were 1,583 gentlemen members and 24 ladies.

The St Andrews Golf Club was founded in 1843 and first called the St Andrews Mechanics Golf Club. Formed by local tradespeople, the 11 founder-members included a cabinet-maker, a mason , a joiner, a tailor, a dancing-master, a butler, a slater, a painter, and a plasterer. It developed as a men-only Club with a Clubhouse overlooking the 18th green and has a current membership of 1,248 plus 179 juniors.

Even older is the all-male Thistle Golf Club comprising 200 artisans, mainly shopworkers. As a result, its main competitions, the Annual General Meeting and the yearly dinner-dance are all held on Thursday afternoons or evenings. It started in 1817 as a Gentlemen's Club, with the leading citizens of St Andrews as its founder-members, and with strict rules on dress and behaviour. These included the need for a uniform green jacket, with black velvet collar and silver buttons with a silver-lace thistle motif, to be worn on the Links at all times and when attending the quarterly meetings. Failure to do so carried a shilling fine and a missing button was charged at 6*d*.

The quarterly subscription was 2*s*.6*d*. and failure to pay it within three days resulted in expulsion – with the need to re-apply for membership at the next quarterly meeting. The winner of the annual competition received a medal, but wasn't allowed to enter for it again for the next four years to give the others a chance. [Try introducing that one among your Club's 'pot-hunters' of today!]

But the well-disciplined, green-jacketed Gentlemen had faded from the scene by 1839, and a new Thistle Golf Club was formed in 1865 from the St Andrews shopkeeping fraternity. It doesn't have a Clubhouse, being now incorporated into the St Andrews Club, but retains its identity because of its colourful and historic beginnings.

The University Golf Club of St Andrews was first mentioned in golfing records when it was named as the home club of Mr P.C. Anderson, who won the British Amateur Championship at Prestwick in 1893.

There are also two Ladies Clubs in St Andrews: St Regulus has about 80 members, and with a Clubhouse on Pilmour Place, about a 7-iron from the first tee on the Old. St Rule's has 177 members and I'd say you'd need a longish putt to make the first tee from the front door of its Clubhouse at 12 The Links.

All the foregoing Clubs list St Andrews Links as their home course, and have separate Standard Scratch Scores for the Old, New, Jubilee, and Eden courses. Their members and guests also need to pay fees and obtain a time from the Starter's Office before they can play on any of them.

That's quite enough history and statistics for a while. Let's return to my arrival at St Andrews.

The Professional Golfers Association produces a directory, annually updated, called *Where to Play and Stay*. Although many hotels are listed in the St Andrews area I hit the bull's-eye with the Scores Hotel, blindly chosen from it when planning the trip. The road outside being almost a cul-de-sac there was no parking difficulty, and from the second floor bedroom window I looked out over St Andrews Bay and the first tee of the Old Course, some 50 paces from the hotel entrance. But 50 paces or 50 miles, I couldn't see my tight schedule of appointments allowing much golfing time.

After a clean-up I got together in the bar with the hotel manager, Tom Gilchrist. Over a 'malt' he had me sign the complimentary copy of the book I'd sent him after our initial chat over the phone the previous week and then ordered 24 copies to sell in the hotel, complete with showcards to display in Reception and the hotel shop. Nice finish to a memorable opening day!

It was as well that I had booked early for my two-night stay, as most St Andrews hotels were filling up rapidly; not so much with tourists, although there was no shortage of them, but starting two days hence was the first of the two R&A member-meetings of the year at each of which a number of Club competitions are held. Members come from all over the world to play and, with something like 400 in attendance, the events are spread over three or four days. At the autumn meeting there are also foursomes- and single-matchplay knockout competitions. A formal dinner ends the festivities, when the new Captain, elected the previous evening, presents prizes.

Despite the number of new arrivals checking in, the dining room of The Scores was almost empty when I wound down with a steak and a bottle of wine, before turning in somewhere around 11 pm. The riveting book brought along for bedtime reading duly riveted for the best part of half a page, before falling from palsied fingers. With just enough presence of mind to reach out and switch off the light, I sank back between luxurious sheets and knew no more.

By 6 am broad daylight had crept through the curtains, St Andrews Bay and the Old Course fairways were bathed in sunshine, and the sight of golfers milling round the Starter's Office and Caddymaster's hut – yes, even at that ungodly hour – had me itching to put Morley foot and clubhead to the hallowed turf.

There was precious little chance of that happening, I learned from the Starter on walking across to his office in the crisp morning air about 20 minutes later. The Old Course was heavily booked with three-and four-balls throughout the day and, in any case, it was not normal practice to waste a precious starting time on a lone golfer when the same slot could accommodate three or four players.

'You're welcome to play the New, Eden, or Jubilee', said the man, but I wasn't interested. It was that evocative 17th hole on the Old I wanted to have a go at so badly, with its challenging drive over the old railway sheds; and if my luck held out, to follow it with a second in the direction of the lozenge-shaped green with its notorious strip of road backing it. And then to stand on the 18th tee and bisect the fairway with a drive just short of the road, cross the little stone humped-back bridge, and power an iron across the 'Valley of Sin' to the very heart of the final green. All the time aware of the excited, milling throng around me (probably have to hire them from Rent-a-Crowd!) and the roar of thousands in my ears.

But as I couldn't expect that phlegmatic Scot to understand the weird workings of a Walter Mitty-like mind, I explained that this was my first time in St Andrews and that as I had to leave again early the following morning, probably never to return, it would have fulfilled the dream of a lifetime – or at least the 30 years of it since first entering the Kingdom of Golf – to have actually played those last two holes. So he kindly suggested that I come down after six that evening, play the first four or five holes going out, and take a chance on finding a gap to cut in on the four-balls wending their way back in the gloaming. Thanking him for his excellent advice I returned to the hotel all het up with anticipation of what was to come at the end of the day and, after a good old Scottish breakfast of porridge and Arbroath smokies, went walk about round the ancient town.

My first call was on Auchterlonie's, an historic corner shop on Pilmuir Links, about a seven-iron from the first tee on the Old Course. It was founded by Tom Auchterlonie, the youngest of six sons of a St Andrews master plumber. The boys learned their golf playing with sticks and corks round the town, using lamp-posts as their targets, with the result that by the time they'd acquired clubs, balls and a few more years, most of them were top-flight players. Willie Auchterlonie won the Open at Prestwick in 1893 and was fifth at St Andrews in 1900 – Taylor, Vardon, Braid, and Jack White taking the first four places. Another brother, Laurie, avoided competing with his brothers by taking up residence as a professional in the United States, where he won the US Open when it was played at a New York course in 1902, after being fourth at Chicago and fifth at Massachusetts in the two previous years. In 1904 and 1906 he was still getting into the frame with a fourth and a third at Illinois clubs.

But it was the brothers Willie and Dave who had the shop with a club-making factory at the back in St Andrews – just a couple of doors up Pilmuir Links from the present shop – where young Tom would mess about with spoiled blocks of wood on his way home from school. He worked at the factory for 22 years, learning the craft, until he started on his own in 1919 – borrowing £200 from a friend in Blackburn at $4^{1}/_{2}$ percent interest to open a shop in the centre of town. At the end of World War Two the business moved to its present site – once the clubhouse of the St Andrews Golf Club – two doors away from the Dave-and-Willie shop and factory where young Tom had served his apprenticeship some 45 years earlier. By this time his son, Eric, had been groomed to take over in due course and the business was named Tom Auchterlonie and Son Limited.

Laurie, son of Willie, was now in control of D. & W. Auchterlonie and wasn't overjoyed at the prospect of family competition on his doorstep. He was a highly-respected figure, whose appointment as Honorary Professional to the Royal and Ancient Club followed that of his father. He was also honoured by the American golf historian, Dawson Taylor, who not only had Laurie write the Foreword to his book, *St Andrews – The Cradle of Golf*, but also had him contribute a full chapter entitled, 'How To Play The Old Course', complete with detailed drawings of each of the 18 holes. Published in New Jersey in 1976, it's a magnificent work dedicated by the author to 'Laurie and Bea Auchterlonie for their friendship and help.'

But there wasn't much friendship between Laurie and his cousin Eric, operating as they did from neighbouring shops about 100 yards from the R&A Clubhouse. It was said that one of them would make a point of checking from his shop window or doorway before leaving for lunch or at the end of the day, just to avoid the embarrassment of coming face-to-face with the other in the street.

When Laurie died in 1988, the 100-year-old business of D. & W. Auchterlonie closed down and the premises acquired by a woollen merchant.

Tom and Eric's famous establishment (on the corner of Pilmuir Links with its entrance now in Golf Place) retains the name and club-making techniques of Auchterlonie's, but now belongs to Gleneagles Golf Products Limited. (No connection with any other firm or place of a similar name!) The company is based at Aladdin's Cave of Golf in Uxbridge, Middlesex. Jim Horsfield is manager at St Andrews and area director of the company. He's been there 17 years and tells many stories going back to the time when Eric Auchterlonie was his boss – like the one about one customer, always anxious that anything he bought should have its Scottish origin patently obvious for all to see, who wrote to order a clubshaft with MacHogany finish!

When I called, the whole of one window featured a detailed mini-layout of craftsmen and workshops as they were at the turn of the century. The shop itself, however,

Tom Auchterlonie's hive of industry in the 1920s.

was well-stocked with modern merchandise to encourage investment in clubs or clothing by those seeking fresh ways to improve their game or charisma. It's also pretty choosey when deciding which golf books to stock and display, but I'm told *By Yon Bonnie Links*! will be among them. Well, they've had about 50 copies of *If it wasn't for Golf . . . !* so far!

Just a few doors along from the Scores Hotel was the HQ of the Ladies Golf Union, where I had an 11 o'clock appointment with the then-acting Administrator. After a friendly greeting and hot coffee, I was taken on a conducted tour of their offices – a large double-fronted house overlooking the Bay – and was shown precious archives going back to its foundation in 1893.

With a full-time staff of four, the LGU regulates conformity among a million or so womenfolk – all named and registered as members of Lord knows how many thousands of Golf clubs in Britain, Ireland, The Commonwealth, South Africa, Europe, and all points East and West. And in some most unlikely places, too.

For instance, it fascinated me to learn there are 16 affiliated Clubs in the Papua New Guinea Ladies Golf Association alone. Hard to reconcile with that notorious Pacific jungle-country where unfriendly natives were obsessed with decapitating anybody they didn't know. With something a lot more messy, that is, than a mis-hit golf shot. Civilisation has much to answer for in destroying long-established impressions of far-away places, as created by the likes of Henty, Ballantyne and Percy Westerman in the books I read as a boy.

The comprehensive 270-page *Handbook* of the LGU proved a mine of information, especially for anyone wanting to know more about Ladies' golf in England, Scotland, Wales and Ireland. (It makes no distinction between the North and

South of Ireland.) In all, 1,961 Clubs are listed, as is the name and Club of every player with a handicap of three or under. From the listings it was nice to see that Michael Bonallack's wife, Angela, is currently playing off 2 at her Scottish Club, Elie, and his sister, Sally Barber, off 1 at Thorndon Park, Essex. That happens to be more relevant than it might seem because they both have a small part in the next chapter – although it's the family men-folk who get star billing in 'The Golfing Bonallacks'.

Bidding farewell to acting-Administrator Alma Robertson, I strolled 100 yards along the sunlit road to the front door of the Royal and Ancient Club of St Andrews for my noon appointment with its Secretary.

But before leaving the LGU completely, I should add that at the time of my visit Alma was looking after things while the regular chief was otherwise occupied – like preparing for motherhood. But mothering was to take precedence over administrating so Alma Robertson was found to be in charge – permanently – when I returned to St Andrews. A native of Aberdeen, with a handicap of nine and two grown-up daughters, she's had an interesting career apart from golf. As an ex-Scottish international hockey player she taught P.E. for five years at St Leonard's Girls School, St Andrews – one of the top private boarding schools in the country, I was told. She had also lived in Australia, Mozambique, and Texas. All of which helped make her a most interesting dinner companion when she joined me and some friends in The Scores Restaurant a year after that first meeting.

—— 6 ——

The Golfing Bonallacks

The start of this book told how Michael Bonallack's invitation to the R&A triggered off my cross-country pilgrimage in the Land of Golf. Before describing the unique nature and contents of this ancient 'Temple', the history of its custodian deserves more than a passing mention.

We first met in 1959, but the family name was familiar since, as an apprentice electrician in 1934, I worked with Supply Company engineers at the coach-building factory of Bonallack & Sons of London, where a small army of skilled craftsmen constructed and fitted timber and metal bodies to commercial vehicles of the era.

On 31 December of that year, a second son was born to Richard, son of Frank Bonallack, one of the partners. The new arrival was named Michael Francis. His elder brother, Anthony, had arrived on Guy Fawkes Day three years earlier, and sister Sally was born in April 1938.

It wasn't until February 1990 that, when putting this story together, I learned enough of its background to justify giving the House of Bonallack its own chapter. The occasion was a fact-finding mission to Michael's father, 86-years-old Sir Richard Bonallack, CBE (Military) ('Call me Dick', he said, on opening the door) at his home adjoining Thorpe Hall Golf Club, of which he is President and where he once played down to four handicap. He still enjoys a couple of rounds a week.

Clutching a liberally-poured Scotch (but well watered down it being a good 45 miles straight back on the M25 afterwards) I was welcomed by three generations of Bonallack: Sir Richard; Michael's elder brother, Tony, whom I knew well and about whom more later; and Tony's 14-year-old son, Steven. Having got off school that morning with a dental appointment, he had used the opportunity to pop into grand-dad's on the way back and hear family history unfolded for this pal of his dad, currently researching on his famous uncle for a new book.

The name Bonallack is that of a hamlet in Cornwall on the Helford River, near Helston, which in turn took its name from the Bonallack ancestral home. For hundreds of years the principal means of livelihood, apart from farming, was tin- and china clay-mining. Then, with the introduction of Customs Duties, smuggling became a profitable activity, with the advantage of working in the fresh air instead of grubbing about below ground. So Cornish folk went for it in a big way.

John Bonallack, then the village squire, tried his hand at it and was quite successful. Being a deeply religious man, he concentrated on the illegal import of 'holy water' – in the shape of fine brandy and rum – and was said to have donated much of the proceeds to the church. Finding that the Revenue enforcement officers were unable to curb John's entrepreneurial activities, the authorities sent in a regiment of Dragoons to stamp them out.

One night John returned from one of his 'business trips' to learn that the 'Black Dragoons' – as christened by the Cornishmen – had discovered his stock of smuggled brandy. According to rumours he had it hidden in the crypt

'They be not for playing games ye know – they be meant for bashin' they
accursed Black Dragoons!'

of the local church. Aware that the game was up and arrest imminent, John took his wife, and as much of the illegal stock as could be carried down and stowed on board the boat, and sailed off down the Helford river that same night. He finished up at Sandgate, in Kent, where he sold his cargo of brandy to Jacob, Earl of Radnor, who became his friend and landlord.

In 1793 his wife gave birth to their first child and being a boy he was christened Jacob, after the Earl. A year later a second son, William was born.

For the next thirty years John earned his living by the repair and maintenance of boats, coaches, and wagons, being assisted by his two sons as they grew up. But when his wife died John decided to have another go at his old profession.

His luck finally ran out in 1825, when his boat encountered a coastguard cutter in the Channel, which opened fire when he tried to get away. John and his younger son, William, were killed but Jacob managed to swim ashore.

Deciding that smuggling was a 'health risk' and that there was a better chance of longevity if he stuck to coachbuilding, Jacob walked up to London and set up as 'J. Bonallack, Wagon Builders' in the East End. He chose that area because he wanted to be near the Docks for the commercial business, and near Aldgate, as that was the point from which coaches set out for the towns and cities of East Anglia.

He prospered, moved to larger premises in Cable Street, Shadwell, and changed the business name to Bonallack and Sons when he brought his two boys into the firm. They built good wagons and showed much enterprise. Jacob's second son, Walter (Michael's great grandfather) even went out to America by one of the new trans-Atlantic square-rigged cutters and returned with orders for wagons, some of which took part in the first migration westward across the prairies.

With the advent of the horseless carriage they switched to producing bodywork for petrol-driven commercial vehicles. The firm remained a partnership until 1936, when it became a limited company with Walter Bonallack as Chairman, and Richard, Michael's father as managing director.

Came the War, Richard, and Walter's son Basil, both being members of the Territorial Army, departed for the duration – Basil earning a Military Cross at Dunkirk and Richard a Military OBE for services in the Middle East.

Once hostilities ended they rejoined the old firm and helped its expansion; whereby in 1953 the old factories were disposed of and a large modern one built in the new town of Basildon, Essex. It was therefore a strong and thriving business when young Michael Francis was made a director in 1962, having joined the company six years earlier after an education at sports-loving Haileybury college and two year's National Service as a Lieutenant in the Royal Army Service Corps.

My first meeting with Michael was at Edward Holdright's Indoor Golf School in Regents Park, where I took a course of lessons in 1959 to learn how to hit a ball – as so painfully described in my last book. Michael, and his equally top-golfing wife, Angela, would sometimes be checking in or out of there when I was doing likewise, or else could be heard thwacking balls into the nets of adjoining 'classrooms'. Their faces were already familiar from sporting pages of the day, but Edward would courteously and carefully introduce us each time we met and emphasise how players of even outstanding calibre were conscious of the need for regular tuition.

As a direct result of those meetings – with Holdright, that is, not me – Michael went on to win his first British Championship in 1961; again in 1965 and then three-in-a-row in 1968, 1969, and 1970. Plus the English Championship in 1962 and 1963; followed by almost another three-in-a-row in 1965, 1966, and1968. ('The British' is open to amateurs worldwide; 'The English' is for nationals only). He was awarded the OBE in 1971, Captaincy of the British Walker Cup Team in 1969 and 1971, and the Bobby Jones award for distinguished sportsmanship in Golf in 1972.

When winning the 1968 English title he played David Kelly in the final at Ganton. The latter was shattered by the fact that despite par figures in the 18-hole morning round he was 11 down when they went in to lunch! Michael had shot a 61 – 32 out and 29 back. He won the match 12 up and 11 to play. A record score for an English Championship.

But he achieved so many 'firsts' it's a job to know where to stop. His wife Angela won the Ladies English Championship in 1958 and 1963, as did his sister Sally in 1968. So there's one record of a husband and his wife winning their respective national championships in the same year, and another of a sister and a brother doing much the same thing five years later.

He was chairman of the Golf Foundation from 1977 to 1983, and Chairman of the Professional Golfers Association from 1976 to1982. In 1983 he took over as full-time Secretary of the Royal and Ancient Golf Club of St Andrews.

His 5'6" elder brother contrasts considerable with Michael's 6'1"; but with the shoulder-width of a pocket-Hercules Tony can hit the ball a country mile. Although currently 6 handicap, he was a County player off 1 when in his prime, and captain of Essex in 1969–70. As members of the Eccentric Club Golfing Society, Tony and I often played together, and met twice in the celebrated Silver Owl Match Play Knockout Competition. He slaughtered me the first time when we played at St George's Hill, but I had my revenge a few years later at Thorndon Park where, off 9, I received 6 shots and sank a long putt to pip him on the 18th.

He reached the 36-hole final of the knockout in 1968 and, after being six down at lunch, was back to one down at the 18th, but just couldn't pull it off. Sitting talking about it all in his father's house, he showed me the 5"-high solid silver Owl he received as losing finalist from the Captain of the Eccentric Club at the festivities after the match. The winner's Owl was 10" high and solid silver, too. I mention this because, traditionally, the Captain walks the 36 holes with the finalists as match-referee, and as the Eccentric Club Captain in 1968 happened to be me, I well recalled the 1968 final and Owl-presentation as Tony related his tale.

But the winner of that 10" silver Owl in the ECGS knockout competition that year warrants more than a passing mention. He is William Trevor Warrin, past Chairman of the Eccentric Club, and known throughout English-speaking parts of Pinner – and most other outposts of the country where Golf is spoken – as 'Dickie' Warrin. Built like an under nourished hairpin, his 6-foot frame over the past 50 years has been instantly recognisable in the remotest parts of his own course – or of any he happened to be playing – by a long, loping limp; the result, as a youth, of a skating accident that shattered his hip and sentenced him to countless operations while lying five years in hospital plaster from the waist down, and a life-long diet of painkillers.

Despite the physical limitations he went on to become a full time director of Woolworths and had a practice golf net installed on the flat roof of their HQ in Oxford Street, London. Where he'd spend his lunch sessions hitting hundreds of balls, instead of over-indulging at 'fleshpot dispensaries' as was the wont with we weaker members of the Eccentric fraternity. If only I had followed his example my handicap today – let alone my weight – might be a lot lower than it is. In Dickie's case he was 3 handicap when he played Tony Bonallack for that 1968 silver Owl (He actually won five of them between 1961 and 1981.)

But it was an item in the 1990 Spring Bank Holiday newspapers that had me adding this story to a chapter – and come to that a manuscript – that was already finished and about to go to print. It said that Angela Uzielli had just won the Ladies Amateur Championship for the second time, having set a record by doing so at the age of 50. (A very young and attractive 50, I might add.)

Dickie's son, Steven, is also a top-flight amateur golfer, and with his father won the national Fathers and Sons foursomes knockout in 1974 at West Hill, Surrey. Hundreds enter from all over the country and it takes about a week before the finalists battle it out over 36 holes. After that a man with two good legs would be glad to lay them down for a week, let alone one with a tortuous bobbing-up-and-down gait.

At around the same time there is a similar national Mothers and Daughters competition at a course near by, and that year it was won by Peggy Carrick and her daughter, Angela Uzielli. By tradition the two pairs of winners play a friendly match afterwards (if any match could be considered friendly at that level of play) with the gentlemen making first contact to arrange dates, venue, etc.

Dickie was a bit slow off the mark – that overworked old hip probably still groaning in protest at the thought of further golf after the West Hill marathon – with the result that Peggy Carrick had to ring him. His apologies for failing to make the initial approach were quickly set aside by the good lady and they soon agreed details for the forthcoming meeting.

About to hang up with fond farewells until the day, the lady added, 'Oh, by the way, Dick, what's the handicap position?'

In a slightly patronising fashion Dick answered, 'Well I'm off three and Stevie's scratch.'

'In that case', came the equally patronising reply after a brief pause, 'you get one shot. I'm two and Angela's plus-one.'

Chauvinistic Dickie proudly claimed that he'd never taken a shot from a lady in his life and had no intention of doing so now.

'I'm afraid you've no option', was the calm retort, 'I play strictly to R&A Rules at all times, and those Rules state that with our respective handicaps my daughter and I have to give you and your son one shot – and one shot you'll be receiving from us in our forthcoming match.'

Whether they did or not is irrelevant – knowing Dick he probably had a deliberate air-shot, while his gallantry wouldn't let him tell me the result – but I always treasured that tale ever since he recounted it round the Club bar several 'yonks' ago!

Back to the Bonallack saga. The Eccentrics would meet monthly at one of the better-known courses around London. The meetings were usually zestful and rich with good fellowship. During his heyday, Michael Bonallack came to one at Royal Wimbledon as a guest of his brother Tony, or possibly one of his Thorpe Hall friends who also happened to be Eccentric members. My friend Reg Davies – who somehow gets himself a bit of mileage in almost anything I write! – was my guest. (Remember, I was his when given that wonderful story of the Horrible Company of Cambridge Golfers at the end of Chapter 5). He played well that morning – well, he always did against me – and came in with 38 points; but protested that as he had won the guest's prize last time he'd be most embarrassed to be called up to collect another one today and asked me not to put his card in. Ignoring his noble sentiments, I persuaded him to sign it, did so myself as marker, lodged it with the Secretary, and in we went to lunch.

At the end of the afternoon round came the usual festive activity around the bar, during which time Reg wandered across to where the Secretary was checking and finalising the score cards in preparation for prize-giving by the Captain. They were out of earshot but it was obvious from the earnest way he was talking that Reg was pleading not to be declared the winning guest this time as it was all too embarrassing. Just as earnestly the Secretary seemed to be having difficulty in telling Reg his fears were groundless and showing some cards to prove his point. Back came my man in a minor state of shock and said;

'I feel a right idiot now, although I'm still to get a prize for being third. I lost it on the back nine for second place, but the winning guest was Michael Bonallack with 45 points, off plus 4! He went round in 61 – a course record, had it been off the back tees!'

Mind you, there's another record of sorts, as told by Tony. It seems that one year he and Michael were each playing in the national Championship, in which the early rounds are over 18 holes. Some fellow put Tony out before lunch, was drawn to play Michael in the next round, and put him out after lunch. Tony said that has to be some kind of record: two brothers each being beaten by the same chap on the same day! He believed the fellow's name was Dunn, but as the man didn't get much further in the competition after his one memorable day, couldn't remember much more about him. Pity really, because that was no mean achievement and worth recording – even if only in this chronicle.

Looking ahead, there are still a few more golfing Bonallacks in the pipeline. Michael's son, Robert, is 23 years old and plays to single figures; and Tony's son, Steven, is coming along fast. His grandfather told me proudly that Steven, currently off 16, and Tony won the afternoon scratch round last year of the Chigwell Open Family Foursomes. [*Stop press: Steven cut to 8 hcp Aug. 1990!*] Nevertheless it hasn't gone to his head and he feels there's still some way to go before he shatters his uncle's tally of titles!

Once with a handicap of three but now 9, Michael's eldest daughter, Glenna, also spends her working day in a world of golf. She is secretary to Alex Hay, managing director of Woburn Golf and Country Club, author of countless books and magazine articles – not to mention the Foreword to my last book – and BBC Television Golf commentator.

Another daughter, Sara, looks after the catering for IMG, the company owned by Mark McCormack, mega-manager to countless sports celebrities, including many world-famous golfers. A third daughter, Jane, however, is a farmer's wife and probably more inclined to look on grassland as grazing rather than golfing country.

The timing of my Scottish expedition had been aimed at linking the chance of some half-decent travelling weather with Michael's return from the Augusta Masters. Although many well-known faces are often noticed when the action is screened from Augusta, he usually manages to maintain a pretty low profile while renewing old friendships and providing decision back-up when needed at the major international events.

But in April 1989, millions of TV viewers witnessed his involvement in a bit of instant decisioning at a vital point in the fourth day's play. For those who didn't it went something like this. Having hooked his tee-shot into the crowd lining the fairway of the 10th hole, Seve Ballesteros claimed that his ball was lying in badly-trampled ground and merited a free drop. The official on the spot agreed but Seve's playing partner, Ken Green, didn't, and asked for a second opinion. Play was held up for about 20 minutes, with cameras showing plenty of action elsewhere around the course and returning periodically to the inaction around Seve's ball.

Then the commentator said that 'no less than the top man from the R&A, Michael Bonallack himself, was on his way over to adjudicate'. Came his eventual arrival on the scene, it took but one quick look, precious little deliberation, and no discussion whatsoever with anybody else around, for him to point dispassionately with his furled umbrella for the ball to be played from where it had been lying for the best part of half an hour. Likewise, with no hesitation – or discomfiture – Seve Ballesteros walked up to it, took his stance, and calmly rifled a 'screamer' in the general direction of the green!

Can't remember how all that 'palaver' affected his partner's play for the rest of the round, but 'Mr Gamesmanship' – as more and more sports' writers tend to call the great Spaniard – seems to thrive on controversial issues that would make lesser mortals like you and me blush to the roots of our hair with embarrassment. Well, certainly me, and with the amount of hair I'm crowned with today that would be no mean achievement!

— 7 —

St Andrews – 2

With the influx of Members arriving for the spring meeting referred to earlier, the entrance lounge of the R&A clubhouse was a-buzz with meetings-and-greetings, while I waited for Michael to arrive in answer to the hall-porter's call. He then took me on a tour or the 135-year-old building, with its vast array of trophies and colourful links with the history of the game.

At the time of writing this chapter, newspapers and golf magazines were full of a claim for many millions of dollars against the R&A and the USGA made by the manufacturers of Ping clubs. They objected to having a range of their products declared illegal by both authorities on the game. Something about the number and shape of groovings in the clubface. Well, there's nothing new about that sort of situation up at St Andrews judging by the range and variety of old, and not-so-old, illegal clubs I was shown on display in glass cases. Each had a label giving the reason for rejection and each, no doubt, sold in quantity before crestfallen manufacturers found their latest gimmick for the golf-addicted market had 'laid an egg'.

It came as a great surprise, when admiring the massive Amateur Championship Cup, and also the silver Claret Jug presented to the winner of the Open each year, to learn that they both sit permanently – beautifully polished and engraved – behind the locked glass doors of a first-floor trophy cabinet. They never leave it. Those we see presented each year and held aloft by jubilant victors are replicas, made to order for the presentation and identical to the originals in every way, right down to the last winner's name engraved on the side or plinth.

From Michael's spacious office-cum-Committee Room on the second floor the panoramic windows and balcony provided a commanding view of all four courses and St Andrews Bay. Judging by the sets of powerful binoculars and telescopes on swivel stands bolted to the floor at those windows, very little taking place out on the Links would escape eagle-eyed observers keeping a watching brief over the scene; and woe betide the miserable competitor dropping a crafty second ball when somewhere out in the country to replace the one he'd lost.

Writing of those unseen watching eyes brings to mind the story of an American competitor having a practice round, accompanied by a local caddy, before the 1989 Dunhill Masters. Landing his approach shot on one of those vast double greens and a long, long way from the hole he was attacking, the player studied the situation and then asked for his seven iron. The caddy hesitated. Impatiently, the aspiring Master asked if there was some local rule about taking an iron from the edge of the green when that far from the hole. 'Ah dinna ken ef there's ony rule – but ef ye took yon iron Ah doot ef they'll let ye play here agen!'

In contrast to the four full-time officials at the Ladies Golf Union, Mike has a staff of 23 to help run the R&A as an international ruling body, and a similar number taking care of the Club and Clubhouse matters.

The daily postbags bulge with requests for decisions on obscure interpretations of the Rules of Golf. They come from

You sure nobody's watching?

Clubs and groups all over the world – including, no doubt, Papua New Guinea! Annually the queries and answers are bound into the *Joint Decision Book on the Rules of Golf*, published by the R&A and the USGA, and bought by Golf Unions, Club Secretaries and the like; on the basis that by reference to it a parallel case-history and decision can be found without having to go to the 'Appeals Court' for a ruling on some new, or what turns out to by not-so-new, issue.

Yet they keep coming in. I have a copy of the 1988 *Decision Book*, containing nearly a thousand such decisions, and about the size of Tolstoy's *War and Peace*! Just about as violent, too, when you read between the lines and realise how good friends must have reached the pistols-at-dawn stage over some of the unbelievably petty disputes. Nevertheless some of us still believe that if played with true sportsmanship the game wouldn't need much more than half-a-dozen guide lines on a single sheet of paper.

Later, I phoned to ask Michael if he had a recent way-out example of 'decisioning' that might suit this story. He told of one from the United States concerning a lady professional in a competition. It went something like this:

Playing a particular hole with a lot of water around it her shot landed safely on the green. She put a marker in the turf and, without looking round, picked the ball up and tossed it nonchalantly in the direction of the caddy for the usual cleaning routine. The sort of thing witnessed all too often on TV as performed by flamboyant louts, and aped by many who should know better. [*My comment, not Michael's.*]

Only this time the caddy was caught unawares and the ball sailed past into the deep blue waters of the lake. After much frantic and abortive 'fishing' the by-this-time-not-so-flamboyant lady was obliged to put down another ball by her marker and putt out.

By so doing, ruled the R&A and the USGA she was in breach of Rule 15-1, which says a player must hole out with the ball played from the tee, unless another Rule allows substitution of the original one. As there isn't a Rule permitting balls to be tossed nonchalantly into deep lakes, she incurred a penalty of two strokes in stroke play, or loss of hole in match play!

I bet that lady takes a good look round, or calls her caddy over for a hand-to-hand 'pass', before sending her ball to the 'cleaners' again!

Michael produced the plans for a new and impressive 6,500 square feet St Andrews Museum, the foundations for which are tucked into a sunken portion of Bow Butts, just 50 yards from the Clubhouse. It is so designed that the finished single-storeyed building doesn't obstruct the scenic view of links and ocean from the road close by. The ceremonial opening was planned to coincide with the 1990 Open Championship at St Andrews.

Learning that Scores Hotel had stocked up with 24 copies of my masterpiece he suggested that two other hotels with integral golf shops might be worth a visit. The lady who ran the shop in The Rusacks – a Trust House Forte hotel – said she'd like a little time to think on whether to stock it. [*She's had well over a year so far.*]

The St Andrews Old Course Hotel, or the old version of it, was a familiar sight to all who watched St Andrews golf on TV. It's the one where top players float their drives over two-dimensional imitations of two old railway sheds just inside the perimeter fencing when playing the 17th (Road Hole). Run-down and almost derelict, the hotel was bought for

£7 million by a Japanese company – which planned to spend a further £17 million to make it the 'flagship' of their hotel group. The lavish spending has to be seen to be believed. Ross Furlong, general manager, made no secret of the pride he felt towards his 'flagship' when showing me around some of the completed public rooms. It's the last word in grandeur – or at least it will be once the army of carpenters, plumbers and electricians have finished banging about.

There are those who say the investors will never get their money back – but I don't know. With their own heliport and Edinburgh airport only a 15-minute 'chopper'-ride away, there's little doubt that half the tycoons of Tokyo are putting hatfuls of yen up-front for the package deal of their lives. Although the hotel closed from the autumn of 1989 to the spring of 1990 to allow work to be completed unhindered, a lot of marketing took place throughout the world during that time, aimed at filling rooms once it reopened in time for the build-up towards the 1990 Open.

Well, I drafted those last two paragraphs soon after returning from Scotland in May 1989, but much had changed when, on driving out from St Andrews to Musselburgh on 1 June 1990, I called there again to find they needed rewriting. But on second thoughts they were left in to show what can happen to factual data even while the ink is still drying. With information gleaned from the newly-appointed Marketing Manager, and the handsome sheaf of publicity material he provided – matched only by the opulent grandeur of the biscuit-coloured stonework of the building itself – here are the relevant points in sequence:

1. The Japanese investment now seems to have become one made by an international consortium called 'The Old Course Limited' made up of the Royal and Ancient Golf Club; a London-based merchant bank, Robert

Fleming and Company; a trust of the Rockefeller family; another of the Oppenheimer family; and the Japanese Seiyo Corporation.

2.   The sum being spent on the project is now quoted as £15 million.

3.   Ross Furlong is no longer general manager, having been replaced in January by Peter Crome, previously manager of the Savoy, London.

Some still express doubts whether this powerful group of investors is likely to get its money back. But with 125 rooms and rates running between £110 and £500 a night (you get a two-bedroom suite for the latter) and already fully-booked for many weeks either side of the forthcoming Open, it's my belief the Dom Perignon corks will be popping with gay abandon in the Boardroom at their next AGM!

It's a dream of a hotel and puts St Andrews, at last, on a par with Gleneagles and Turnberry as far as flagship-status of a top golfing resort-hotel is concerned. And coming later than the other two, both of which have spent themselves silly trying to enhance what are basically 70- and 90-year-old buildings respectively, I'd say the Old Course Hotel is a stroke-up on them, rather than level par!

If in doubt, send off for its marketing pack – that's free, even if its charges don't happen to be in your favourite price range – and stand by for a long drooling session when it arrives!

Taking the story back to that first visit to the Old Course Hotel in 1989, I was introduced by Ross Furlong to John Philp, the ex-golf professional running the hotel golf shop (I understand he's no longer there, either) who stocked up with six copies of my book. Well-sated by this time with a morning's socialising, researching and selling, the time had come to hit the road again: although scheduled to return to base a few hours later.

8

Carnoustie

After a quick salad lunch in The Scores buttery, I drove out over the Tay Toll Bridge (30p, but not as picturesque as its 40p equivalent over the Forth) to Carnoustie, where Henry Cotton won the second of his three Open Championships in 1937, and Ben Hogan his only one in 1953.

On his return to New York, Ben was given a hero's welcome, with ticker-tape raining down from skyscraper windows as he was driven through cheering hordes to the City Hall. Full of emotion he stood on the steps and told them all through the microphone, 'I owe it all to God – and my wife, Valerie!' Nothing about the hundreds of thousands of balls he'd knocked up and down practice fairways throughout his dedicated career.

It's quite a few years now since anybody has had the chance to imply divine help, or publicly thank "er-indoors', for pulling off the big one at Carnoustie. Last held there in 1975, when Tom Watson won it, there's no record of his making Hogan-like proclamations to cheering multitudes on his return to the 'Big Apple'.

There are hardly a dozen hotels in Carnoustie, a pretty little resort town on the east coast, just north of the Tay estuary. I'm told the largest has 10 rooms. Carnoustie was taken off the roster for Open Championship venues after 1975, due to lack of suitable accommodation in the area capable of handling the quantity of 'pilgrims' the event draws today.

But two international groups are each due to build a large luxury hotel close to the Links, and have them ready in time for the Amateur Championship to be played there in 1992. It won't be too long after that, we all hope, that the Open Championship will follow suit and return to one of its most popular venues.

Carnoustie Golf Links consist of three 18-hole courses on land owned by the Angus County Council and on which any may play on payment of the green fee. They are leased to a Management Committee made up of two members from each of the six major golf clubs based at Carnoustie – five male and one female. Club members and the general public book times and pay green fees at the Starter's office on the ground floor of a two-storey building near the first tee. The remainder of that floor is taken up by the administrative staff of the Management Committee and one of the six clubs occupy the upper floor.

But many members of Carnoustie-based Clubs, as with those at St Andrews, who are obliged to share public but prestigious links with all and sundry, also have membership of other Clubs where – even if their playground is a little less illustrious – they do have the exclusive use of their own course.

All this I learned during and after my visit, which began when entering the highly polished but sepulchrally-silent premises of the Carnoustie Golf Club, across the road from the links. Looking around I located a solitary figure in the locker room and asked where I might find Mr Smith. He didn't know a Mr Smith but said the Club Secretary, Mr Curtis, worked from the Starter's office and pointed me in the direction of the two-storey building, about 150 yards from where we stood. Being a lovely day I didn't mind the stroll across the sward, but felt for anybody choosing to do so in a torrential downpour with a force-eight gale blowing in from the North Sea.

Mr Curtis was seated at an open window with the booking register in front of him – I learned later that he doubled his job as the Carnoustie Club Secretary with part-time Starter at the links – and explained that my Mr Smith was Secretary of the Management Committee working from next door.

Which is where I found him, with the kettle on and the book I'd sent a week earlier open on his desk and awaiting the promised signature. An interesting hour ensued while I learned how the place ticked and of its anxiety to regain historical recognition as a world-class tournament centre. But with so much past history to its credit there has never been any shortage of touring golfers around. American accents abounded among the folks signing up to play on the links and in the two shops I visited on the road leading back from the links to the main highway.

9

St Andrews – 3

Tayside in Dundee once bustled with shipping and activity, but it's all gone. As I drove by on my way to and from Carnoustie the docks area was silent and its harbour installations black with rust. Taking a last sad look from the other side of the Toll Bridge at what was once a major British port, it was well after 6pm by the time I reached the Scores Hotel. Time to try my luck on the Old Course.

The duty Starter told me pretty much the same as his colleague had done that morning about going out by myself on the Old, but when I explained what I hoped to do, and why, he just told me to go right on out there and enjoy myself. On the house too! Waiving any fee, as the light would never last to get in anywhere near a full round, he suggested I played about four holes and then cut across to play the last four back.

I couldn't believe my luck as I walked across the springy turf to the empty first tee, blissfully aware of benign fairways smiling at me under the setting sun. Despite a poor second finishing up in the Swilken after a satisfactory drive, it felt an honour to be fishing my ball out of that illustrious burn. Especially when sinking a 40-foot putt after pitching-up from the water's edge. Triumph in making that putt was short-lived, as a wrong line was chosen for a good drive on the second, and the ball lost for ever in thick-tufted rough. Having reached the fourth green with some reasonable golf I walked across to the 15th tee. A four-ball was well down the fairway and, looking back, another could just be seen 500 yards away assembling for their tee shots on the 14th.

The gap was just made-to-measure for me to slot into. But it was all too good to last. Beyond the 16th green was the 17th tee – the dog-legged start of the infamous Road Hole. Approaching, it seemed that everybody out on the course that day was milling around and waiting to play it.

Each four-ball would assemble on the tee, post a look-out about 50 yards out to the left, and hit off once those in front were known to be approaching the green. As they passed out of sight round the corner featuring the imitation railway sheds the next lot of budding 'Faldoes' would get in position and do the same thing. It was ludicrous. I must have watched a dozen drives while waiting there, and most of those that didn't hit the 'sheds', or sail out of bounds behind the hotel boundary fence, finished up 'sprayed' between 20 and 150 yards from the tee. Yet all waited until it was safe to rifle a 300-yarder across the corner to the green.

When it was eventually my turn to put a ball down, the four-ball that was over 500 yards behind when I stood on the 15th tee were now putting-out 20 yards away on the 16th green. I had no option but to ask their approval to play on, bearing in mind that I had no standing as a 'loner' and, in addition, had cut in.

Unfortunately, they were boorish, and English. Two said reluctantly to go ahead, but a third complained that with the light failing they might not be able to finish their game if they had to wait for me. It wasn't true, but not seeking to discuss it further, and with another four-ball approaching,

I shouldered my bag without further ado and trudged down the path leading from the tee, round the hotel perimeter fencing, along the infamous Road (once the railway footpath terminating at St Andrews station) watched a bit of putting out on the 18th, and finally put the clubs in the car. But there was at least one heart-warming feature to the start of that walk.

Having had my dreams of playing those last two holes so cruelly shattered, instant consolation was at hand in hearing not one, but two of the drives from the four-ball behind come to grief against the 'shed' walls soon after turning the corner, and – even better – seeing a third splash into a large ornamental lily pond occupying most of the hotel forecourt. I remember gleefully hoping the latter was old 'Failing - light's' shot, and thanking the 'Great-Golfer-In-The-Sky' for being so quick off the mark with His retribution!

Soaking in the bath, I resolved to get up early on the morrow and try doing the same eight holes again; knowing that once away, the four holes back from the 15th would be empty. But like all good intentions it faded and died when morning arrived. That old bed was far too cosy, despite the outlook being every bit as inviting as on the previous day. A lot of travelling demanded a good start, and an early eight holes could well strain the programme. Anyway that was my excuse for another 40 minutes tucked between the sheets.

Checking out before 8am, I stopped for a cup of coffee in the hotel Buttery, and was asked by an American if I wasn't the same guy he saw showing a book to the manager of a golf shop in Carnoustie, where he happened to be browsing around yesterday. Quite flattering. Especially when I explained and he went out to buy a copy from Reception for me to sign.

Before leaving St Andrews, and just to show how that 17th plays on the minds of the best golfers, I read in a magazine that Tom Kite and Mark Calcavecchia were discussing how to tackle it when planning their play for a recent competition.

'You need to play a big swooping hook,' said Mark, 'and bounce the ball up on to the green.'

And you've got that shot?' queried Tom.

'Yeah, I've got that shot,' replied the other reflectively, 'but I never know when!'

10

Blairgowrie

En route to Blairgowrie, first of four Clubs celebrating centenaries in 1989, I dropped off books ordered during the previous day's walk about into two general bookshops in the centre of St Andrews. Heading out towards the Tay Road Bridge, I took one last admiring look at the Clubhouse, Starter's office and the first tee with its milling throng of golfers and caddies – and a longing one at that old 17th green as I sped by.

The sight of that crowded first tee of the Old brought to mind the story sent me by fellow Golf Collectors Society member, Group Captain Alan Jackson. He was stationed at RAF Leuchars back in 1980 and played his golf at St Andrews where, he wrote,

> The links are very busy in the summer, with many foreign visitors who want to play the Old Course, some of whom hardly know the rudiments of the game. Although there was a strict balloting for start times, those of us from Leuchars were usually 'slipped in' since the then-starter had previously worked in Officers' Mess at Leuchars, and his 'pension' included a bottle of whisky each month from the Mess cellar. One day we were by the first tee waiting to follow three

very portly and very loudly-dressed Italian gentlemen, all of whom appeared to have difficulty in seeing the ball at the address position. The first man topped his ball violently and it came to rest some fifty yards down the middle. The second, after an airshot, trundled his ball some forty to fifty yards to his left front. The third took up a rigid stance, stared at his ball for a full five seconds, and proceeded to hit it at right angles, past the Starter's Box, across the path and deep into the notorious 'Himalayas'.

One of the three caddies, a small wizened man, the colour of mahogany and with a cigarette consisting mainly of two inches of ash dangling from his lips, turned to his companions and said, mournfully, 'Ah weel, it's gaun tae be a long *-ing day, the day!'

Crossing the Bridge and once away from the city centre, I headed north-west through Dundee along semi-deserted roads, until a little under an hour after leaving The Scores, and after a U-turn and 4-mile slog back to a junction where the stupid car had forked up the wrong road, the signposts said I had reached Blairgowrie – 16 miles north of Perth and 'gateway to The Highlands.' Conveniently, the Golf Club was a mile or so to the south of the city, which meant there was no reason to push on into town and start asking its whereabouts. Here's its history.

The Marquis of Lansdowne was Viceroy of India when he wrote to his mother from Government House, Calcutta, in 1889. Apparently the dowager Marchioness was having difficulty managing the family estate back in Perthshire, so he advised that she lease off 42 acres for the construction of a golf course by local enthusiasts in exchange for a rental price of £25 a year.

At that time the game was becoming increasingly popular, with a spate of course-building taking place throughout the British Isles, although both Amateur and Open Championships were still being won mainly by those dwelling north of the Tweed.

Citizens of Blairgowrie and the rural gentry were circularised, and a Major Peter Chalmers – distinguished soldier and all-round sportsman – seems to have been largely responsible for getting the thing off the ground. In an announcement displayed in the *Blairgowrie Advertise*r ('The Blairie') membership was offered for an entrance fee of ten shillings, and an annual subscription of the same amount. What the advertisement did not say was that members, once elected, would be expected to get their coats off and help convert 42 acres of heathery moor into a nine-hole golf course, complete with teeing areas and numbered flags in prepared holes on hand-mown greens. (Can't see a lot of enthusiasm for that sort of thing among the £1,000-plus a year members of Wentworth today.)

There's no record of outside expertise being called in to design the layout of those nine holes but the enthusiastic amateurs responsible won praise indeed for their efforts when Old Tom Morris came across from St Andrews and, having played an inaugural fourball over nine holes with Major Chalmers, the Captain, and the Secretary, declared it the most beautiful inland 'green' (course) he'd ever known; and by that time he'd been instrumental in designing quite a few in several parts of the country. Having appointed a sole agent at a Blairgowrie stationer's for the sale of his clubs, balls and accessories, he billed the new Club £1.14s.1d. for 'Advice on golfing greens and other expenses incurred in coming to Blairgowrie', and, once paid, caught the train back to St Andrews the same evening. [I'm told you'll *never* get the top course-design consultants – like Jack Nicklaus or John Jacobs – to come out for that sort of money today!]

The nine-hole Lansdowne Course – named after the noble family from whom the land was rented – was formally opened on 6 June 1889.

The Spring Meeting followed soon after, when Major Chalmers was rewarded for the enterprise shown in starting the Club by achieving the first course record of 45 strokes over 9 holes. He probably started celebrating his success too early because, the competition being over 18 holes, he clocked 52 in the second round and a Mr Luke is shown as having won the first 18-hole Blairgowrie Golf Club competition.

The records state that 22 competitors took part in that first event and the highest score was 224! (What a lovely day those playing behind that one must have had!). In the Spring Meeting of the following year the same player went round in 167, thereby improving his game by 57 shots in one year!

Within the next two years a Pavilion was built, incorporating 20 lockers, at a cost of £70 (£30 over budget – says the excellent Club centennial history book I was given by its Secretary – which involved borrowing at 4½ per cent interest). New 15-square-yard greens were laid, the course was fenced in, teeing platforms constructed, and a horse-drawn roller purchased with rubber shoes for the horse. 'When needed, horse to be provided by reigning Captain', said the minutes.

As some members were obliged to commute from outlying parts of the surrounding countryside, the Club provided a stable at the back of the Pavilion and charged £1 for life-use, 2/6d for one year, and 6d for the day. But the Captain was allowed 'free parking' as his perks!

Like the old Masonic golfers, Blairgowrie Golf Club wanted its members properly dressed when on parade, and a scarlet coat with green collar, together with brass buttons

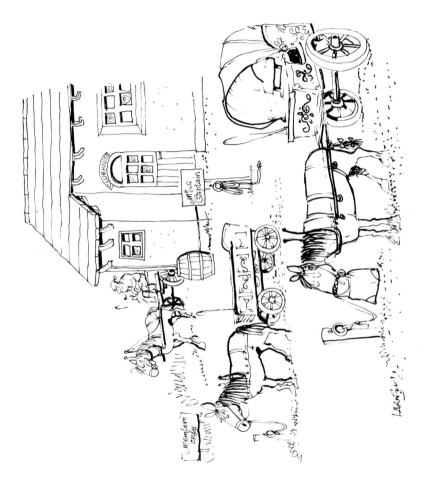

Car(t) Park, Blairgowrie G.C., c1891!

bearing the raised letters BGC engraved thereon, was minuted as the Club uniform for special occasions.

In June 1889 Major Chalmers put the following article in 'The Blairie' under 'Advice to Beginners':

Keep the Rules in your pocket as well as in your head. Frequently read and discuss them especially with experienced players. When in doubt refer to the Rules and play strictly to them. Remember that golf is a game in which the player is strictly on his honour as a gentleman. On medal days, have a previous arrangement against whom you are to play, carry a pencil and mark his score with care.

Be careful in the formation of your style, as it is difficult to cure a faulty style once acquired. Keep your temper. Keep silence and stand quite still while your opponent is addressing the ball. Don't press. Play with easy swing and keep your eye steadfast on the ball until it is away. Mark carefully where your ball drops and keep your eye on the spot until you reach it, when it will be more easily found.

Carry not less than four clean white balls. It is an excellent plan to carry a bit of damp sponge or rag to keep them white. Keep your clubs in order and always clean. Irons should be cleaned with emery paper and sometimes a little oil. A golfing coat should be loose and easy around the shoulders. Braces should be yielding; some players wear none.

Lastly, clip this out and preserve it.

Except for the emery bit there's not many of us around a hundred years later who wouldn't improve as either player or sportsman just from following the good Major's advice.

In 1892 Ladies were allowed a limited membership (no play on Thursdays – thereby leaving the course free for shop-keepers on their half-day closing – or on Saturday afternoons) for 7/6d a year, or 4s for any consecutive four months. They were provided with their own Pavilion in 1895. Costing £57 it was obviously not quite as palatial as the £70 one built for the men three years earlier, but judging from its 1918 sepia-coloured photograph in the souvenir history of the Club, with picket-fenced covered-in verandah like a traditional village-green cricket pavilion, it's amazing what £57 would buy in those palmy days. Yet the Club still had to negotiate a £27 overdraft with the bank to pay for it!

Funds needed, but not readily forthcoming for amenities and improvements – like the aforesaid Ladies Pavilion, or 'provision of urinals and washing facilities in the Gents' Pavilion, using rainwater from the roof' – were more than outweighed by the value of costly trophies donated by wealthy sponsors anxious to have their names perpetuated and toasted at formal dinners. Nor was there any shortage of support among the rank and file at organised banquets and functions when it was known that celebrities of some sort were expected to be present. But the merest whisper of a modest levy or increase in subs to make the place a better Club for all and sundry would set off squeals of protest and disapproval that could be heard two counties away. Usually from the same people who had just spent ten times the amount in question on a new outfit for the next Spring Dinner. And that applies to many clubs today, too.

Among the many distinguished visitors in those early days was Freddie Tait, an officer of the Black Watch and reckoned to be one of the greatest Scottish amateur golfers of all time. In 1894 one of his drives at St Andrews was measured as 341 yards 9 inches, and in October 1897 he broke the course record at Blairgowrie over 18 holes with a

70. Fantastic achievements considering the balls and clubs used in those days. Three years later he was dead – shot in the chest leading a charge in the Boer War.

But what a golfing record he left behind: British Amateur Champion in 1896 and 1898; leading Amateur in the Open Championship 1894, 1895, 1896 and 1899; besides numerous competitive Scottish events.

In 1894, the Club – anxious to attract attention to its new leisure amenity from the city folk who came up to Blairgowrie on vacation with their families during the summer months – advertised Ladies and Gents competitions for visitors. Green fees were one shilling a day, or five shillings for a monthly ticket. Caddy fees were sixpence for nine holes and one shilling for 18, plus a ha'penny or one penny respectively as booking fee for the caddymaster!

The twentieth century was ushered in with the new Captain, a Dundee jute manufacturer, being chauffeur-driven to the course in his new De Dion Bouton (the French equivalent of those days – I am told by my son-in-law, a vintage car enthusiast – to today's Rolls-Royce), and the entrance gates had to be widened to cater for this new form of transport. In appreciation he presented the Club with a flagstaff and a Club flag to be flown on special occasions.

World War One interfered with plans for course improvement, and not until 1927 did the widowed mother of the current Marquis agree to sell a further 73 acres of land to the Club. The price of £4,000 included the freehold of the new acquisition plus the original 42 acres for which they had been paying rent for the past 34 years. (When they bought another 100 acres in 1972 from the same source they had to pay £30,000 for them.) But the new land in 1927 was used to extend the original nine-hole Lansdowne to 18 with the help of course-architect Dr Alistair Mackenzie – he who designed the celebrated Augusta, Georgia, among many others.

Then in 1934, after acquiring further land from the adjoining Rosemount estate for a nominal £80, they had James Braid – who had played an exhibition match with Harry Vardon over the original 9-hole course when reigning Open Champion in 1901 – come up from Walton Heath and redesign a layout incorporating both old and new holes, to form both an 18-hole course and one of nine. They named the former 'Rosemount' in appreciation of the landowner's generous gesture, and the nine holes became the 'Wee Course'.

It was said that Braid strode through the heather on arrival and, glancing around and about, put stakes in the ground where he considered each hole should be – stopping only to collect a fee of £10 before catching a southbound train from Blairgowrie station the same evening. Shades of Old Tom Morris 41 years earlier!

Another 6895 yard 18-hole course, designed by David Thomas and Peter Alliss, was officially opened in 1976 and named 'The Lansdowne', with the current Marquis doing the honours.

By this time the full membership was 1,200 and the subscription £50. By 1989 the membership remained the same but the annual fee had increased by 150 per cent to £125. A special reduced membership of the Wee Course only was £62.50. The Clubhouse had been rebuilt a couple of times since that £70 Men's Pavilion of 1890 and a further extension in 1985 made it a most impressive one. By this time, no doubt, both the Men's urinals and ablutions had been linked to piped mountain water, instead of rainwater from the roof denied them by their parsimonious predecessors!

It was obvious when I arrived for my meeting with Secretary/Manager Dennis Kirkland that no expense had been spared over the years to make Blairgowrie Golf Club continue to live up to its entry in the *Golfing Annual* of 1905, in which it is described as 'One of the prettiest greens in Scotland'. Although there are doubts whether the Royal Hotel, recommended in the same *Golfing Annual* entry, still honours the 'Special tariff to Golfers – 10s per day, £2.10s per week. Bus meets arrival of all trains.'

Surrounded by a book-keeper, personal secretary, and all the hardware, software, and trimmings of an Apricot computer in his crowded first floor office, Dennis Kirkland said his Club was one of the biggest employers of labour in Blairgowrie, with a total of 23 full-time staff, plus 7 part-timers during the busy summer months. And that, he said, was without Gordon Kinnoch, the professional, and his staff of three.

For those who enjoy statistics, this 54-hole golfing retreat now covers over 450 acres, including a large lake named 'The Black Loch'. (That's to distinguish it from the 'White' one which lies on the other side of the road to the Blairgowrie complex.) Some indication of the Club's popularity is provided by the fact that it had 11,000 visitors in 1988 paying green fees.

Yes they've certainly come a long way since they rented those 42 acres from the Viceroy of India's mother back in 1889. It was also a pleasing exercise to write about a private golf Club that developed from scratch in a familiar fashion, instead of delving into and trying to fathom out the history of Club-less courses, course-less Clubs, and Club-and-course-less Societies.

Gordon Kinnoch, the Club professional, had celebrated his first 25 years at Blairgowrie three years earlier. The Club presented him with honorary life membership at a dinner to mark the occasion. Looking out over the wooded vista from his well-stocked shop there was no shortage of visitors and members arriving to play, and during the time it took for him to order six copies of my book and me to get them from the car and sign them, he and his assistant had taken eight green fees from sundry visitors, mostly Americans. In fact the place has become so popular that the Committee introduced restrictions for the centenary year in an effort to keep itinerant golfers off the courses. They partially succeeded as there was a $4\frac{1}{2}$ per cent drop in the number of green fees shown in the register for 1989.

However, I was told there would always be room for me, should I ever return with enough time to go out and enjoy their beautiful course.

——11——

Murrayshall

M y next appointment was at Murrayshall Golf Club, about 4 miles north-west of Perth. It was another of those Clubs recommended as celebrating its centenary in 1989 and, unknown prior to the recommendation, it has done little since to help me know it better. In fact Murrayshall has been the big question mark in the book, wrapped in a shroud of mystery right until it came to preparing this chapter almost a year later.

The fact that I hadn't heard of it was no mystery in itself, as the same would apply to a host of excellent Clubs much nearer home than one in Perthshire. But the first mystery came when I phoned to speak to its Secretary, as I had done in all the other cases when planning this trip. But this time I was told they didn't have one – only a professional, Neil Mackintosh, who happened to be out on the course at that moment, teaching. 'Strange,' I remember thinking at the time, 'how can a Club function without a Secretary?', but made an appointment to meet Neil an hour after the one planned with Dennis Kirkland at Blairgowrie.

A 20-minute drive south on the A93 towards Perth, through pretty, undulating countryside, brought me to the second mystery: a sign pointing left and saying 1½ miles to Murrayshall. No mystery about the sign in itself, but despite travelling more than twice that distance along a winding secondary road with scenic beauty on both sides, there was no trace of town, village, or Golf Club called Murrayshall.

After a good 3 miles I stopped on a short stretch of ridge-like road and took in the glorious panoramic views across rock-strewn grazing land below, searching for tell-tale signs of fairways, bunkers or flags.

As luck would have it a Range Rover, or general purpose vehicle of that ilk – the only one of any description seen since turning off the A93 – came chugging up the hill and pulled up. Well, there was little option without risk of toppling off the road in trying to pass me. The driver was a helpful local farmer who, when asked, explained my destination was a couple of miles back on the road we'd travelled, and needed a sharp turn left at a sign pointing to Murrayshall. Thanking him and feeling a right fool at missing it on the way up, I drove on a few yards and found space enough for a U-turn, by instalments, before heading back down hill once he'd got by.

Keeping eyes double-skinned this time, I saw both the turn and the sign in question. Well, I'd seen it the first time but as it only indicated that the road led to 'Murrayshall Hotel' I'd assumed the golf course lay further up the road. But it didn't. It was right at the back of the hotel and didn't even have reference to a Golf Club at its entrance.

Mystery number three was that despite getting on quite well with Neil Mackintosh – who stocked up with six books – I never received any reply to subsequent requests for Club history to help compile this chapter, when writing to them twice over the ensuing nine months. There were, of course, no plans for any writing at the time otherwise there would have been more looking and asking around. But in the absence of information on the mysteries of Murrayshall, it was about to get only the briefest of mentions when the rest of this was almost ready for printing.

Then came a blinding light that dispelled all mysteries, via the March 1990 edition of a golf magazine. Idly riffling through its pages I came to a section headed, 'Golfing in Ireland and Scotland', with a montage of advertisements on one page featuring the most prestigious hotels. And of the seven familiar Scottish names featured – such as Gleneagles, St Andrews Old Course, Greywalls, Turnberry – the one occupying twice as much space as any of the others was Murrayshall Country House Hotel, Restaurant, and Golf Course – Visitors, golf societies, and company golf days welcome'. The penny dropped!

The reason they didn't have a resident Golf Club Secretary was because it wasn't a Golf Club – it was part of the hotel complex. The reason I couldn't find a sign pointing to Murrayshall Golf Club was because it didn't exist as such – it was part of the hotel complex. The reason no information was forthcoming was because I'd written to Murrayshall Golf Club – not the hotel complex.

I don't doubt there's a low-profile Club of sorts, with its own spare-time Hon. Sec. operating from home, made up of people living in the area and who are allowed to play on the hotel's course in a grace-and-favour fashion – much the same as at Turnberry Hotel, Gleneagles, or the RAC Club, Surrey – but with priority of play decided by the hotel management.

So to waste no further time I phoned the manager of the hotel complex. He wasn't available. When told of the purpose of my call the telephone operator said she'd put me through to hotel sales, or marketing, manager. It happened to be a lady on another line at the time, so the operator said she'd get her to call as soon as she came off it. Another mystery then developed, as over an hour and a half went by and she never did. So I called again and was put through to her this time. She sounded terribly efficient. I'd hardly started to explain my reason for calling when she said she'd put a marketing pack in the post which would tell me all.

She needn't have bothered. When it arrived it was merely a number of separately-folded printed sheets of thick paper doing a hard-sell on the hotel amenities as a conference and leisure centre; and listing many of the outdoor activities available, including ballooning! But as they spelt that with just one 'l' it might mean something other than floating round the mountains beneath an inflated gas bag. But there was nothing about the history of the golf course or, come to that, the hotel.

Curiouser and curiouser, I thought, so looked the place up in Donald Steel's *Golf Course Guide to Britain and Ireland.* That told me it was an undulating, parkland 18-hole course designed by J. Hamilton Stutt, and that the Club was founded in 1981! Then where did all this centenary-stuff come from whereby it was included in my trip? Another blinking mystery!

Which means that as the place has already taken up far too much time and effort with virtually nothing to say about it, I shall have to close the Murrayshall saga here and now with the observation that it sits in a beautiful woodland setting, has spectacular views of the Grampian Mountains, and although completely secluded from civilisation, is only 4 miles from the Fair City of Perth.

—12—

Gleneagles

After little more than half an hour along the A9 from Perth I drove into the magnificent Gleneagles Leisure Complex, spread over 750 acres, and pulled up at the canopied entrance to the hotel building.

'Call me John', said the burly, bare-kneed, John 'The Greeter' McGillivrey, as he came forward to open the driving door. With a firm handshake, plus a bit of prompting, he told me of his 47 years with the Gleneagles Hotel, mostly spent in welcoming guests on arrival, relieving them of car keys, and parking their vehicles once he'd supervised unloading of bags by the hall staff. His traditional cloak, bonnet and kilt were in the colours of the Gleneagles tartan, specially designed for this sumptuous Highland oasis many years ago. [Curiously, there was no mention of a house-tartan in the vast array of four-colour literature I was given on the place. I would have thought they'd have used it to decorate some of their pages. Though one booklet does show a long shot of the hall-porter's desk with what looks like the kilted John standing beside it.]

My room wasn't quite ready, they said, and a large party of Americans – or was it Japanese? – were milling around the spacious reception lounge and only half-way through checking out.

Gleneagles Hotel.

From a 1930 picture postcard. The croquet lawn is now a putting green, and there is a second row of dormer windows in the mansard roof.

Thanks to excellent world-wide marketing techniques, the golfing 'Meccas' of Gleneagles, Turnberry, Troon and St Andrews could well be responsible for as much of our foreign-currency earnings as North Sea Oil and ICI put together. Nevertheless, each of the big hotels I visited on this trip gave the same impression of wanting to play down reputations as international golfing resorts and to develop stronger images of luxury leisure centres in their own right, seeking to attract more non-golfing, wealthy travellers, and top business houses seeking up-market venues for their conferences.

Gleneagles even gave its name to that infamous Commonwealth Conference of 1982, whereby our South African friends were barred from competitive sport, while a blind eye was turned on the internal racial practices of so many of those member-nations passing judgement on our erstwhile allies.

Although golf has always been the most popular and well-known of the ever-increasing number of Gleneagles amenities, its origins go back only as far as the end of our twentieth century Edwardian era – not to the pre-Stuart and early Georgian days of golf as featured in previous chapters.

In 1910, says the Gleneagles marketing literature, Mr Matheson was general manager of the Caledonian Railway Company. He enjoyed a holiday in the valley of Strathearn to such an extent that he went back and told his Board that he'd found them a gold mine. All it wanted, he said, was a palatial hotel built with first class golfing amenities, designed to suit a natural setting of pine, heather, gorse, hills, glens, and sparkling water – against a backdrop of Grampian Mountains to the north and, on a fine day, Ben Lomond to the west – and lucrative trade would just roll in from the wealthy travelling classes throughout the land.

Not only did the board of the Caledonian Railway believe all their manager said, but wasted little time in acting on his words. A company called 'Gleneagles Ltd' was formed in 1913, once all the technicalities and legalities of the project were finalised, with the Railway as the major shareholder.

Well, that's the sort of story the Gleneagles marketing literature dramatically unfolds. What is much more likely is that the Caledonian saw what a rival Scottish company, the Glasgow and South Western Railway, had achieved when acquiring the Marquis of Ailsa's private golf course at Culzean in 1901 and opening it up as the luxury Turnberry complex in 1906 (see Chapter 15). This caused other railways to gnash teeth in envy and cast around in their own territories for an opportunity to do something similar. But even in those golden days it still took time, enthusiasm and money to plan routes, negotiate wayleaves, and placate conservancy interests, even once a site had been found and approved by all concerned. That's probably why it wasn't until 1913 that the Gleneagles project got under way. There's also the possibility that they dragged their heels a bit – bearing in mind the ambitious plan was going to need a lot of finance – until the publicity and success achieved by Turnberry in 1912, when it hosted the British Ladies Amateur Championship, started another bout of teeth-gnashing at the 'Cally' HQ. Word went out to get the Gleneagles show on the road without further delay.

'Let's waste no more time and get down to beating those West coast boys at their own game,' was probably the cry, 'and any funds we need can be raised in the stock market.' And so it came to pass.

But 1913 wasn't too good a year to start anything, followed as it was by 1914 and World War One. The half-finished project was abandoned and not until 1922 was work recommenced on the scheme, with Mr Matheson – the original general manager – still in charge of the operation. During this period it came under the control of London Midland and Scottish Railway, both The Caledonian Railway Company and Gleneagles Ltd having been acquired by the LMS in 1923. Little time was wasted in making up for the lost years, and with a fanfare of publicity and hype The Gleneagles Hotel was opened in June 1924.

'The Playground of the Gods', as one national paper called it when reporting on its grand opening, set standards hitherto unknown. Gossip columnists itemised statistics as though for a *Guinness Book of Records:*

> In-house cold storage plant and bakery with all cooking and baking done by electricity.
> Automatic potato-peelers and egg-boilers, plus dish-washers that could handle 2,000 items an hour.
> Two hundred and sixteen luxury bedrooms and seating capacity in the dining room for 300 guests at small tables, where diners could choose their fish course swimming around in strategically-placed aquariums (the fish, that is, not the diners!).
> Twelve miles of multi-coloured deep-piled carpets.
> Space for 200 couples to dance on the ballroom floor, where Henry Hall, aged 26, and his Orchestra made their BBC début from Gleneagles on that opening night, and thereafter twice weekly for many years to come.

A couple flew their private plane up from Suffolk on a weekend jaunt and landed on the golf course after a three-hour-and-forty-minute flight; about as long as it now takes Concorde to fly from Heathrow to New York – or a would-be 'Concordist' to drive, park, and board when travelling from Central London to Heathrow!

Another flew on his own from Croydon to join his parents for lunch; and yet another made the headlines having raced his Rolls-Royce to Gleneagles and beaten the express train from London by ten minutes, despite stopping three times for meals.

The national press and quality magazines never tired of this type of news snippet or feature which, had they occurred elsewhere, wouldn't have rated more than couple of lines at the foot of an inside page of a local 'rag'. But Gleneagles was Britain's Hollywood-cum-Royal-Ascot from the word 'Go!'

Society columns raved about Americans with their own cars arriving there in droves from liners docking at Glasgow. The White Star Line put display advertisements in the top US journals with photographs of the Gleneagles golfing scene, as featured on the next page.

Meanwhile in the *Westminster Gazette* an observer wrote:

I cannot tell you half the ritualistic things people do here. They tea-dance in the gayest of sun lounges with windows open to the Ochill Hills and the glen. They mix-bathe in the swimming pool in costumes of Deauville splendour. They play billiards and bridge and dance again in the ballroom of mirrors and gilt chairs and stage decorated with Japanese trellis.

Then, exultant from the dance, they midnight bathe in the pool again under lamps that give a light white as sunlight. At the windows they smoke a pyjama-cigarette, [was that some élite brand?] with the wine-like air from the Perthshire hills and the night and the stars playing about them.

All a bit corny for the gossip columns and travel brochures of this day and age, but pretty mind-boggling for the open-mouthed unsophisticate of the 1920s.

THE GREEN/ AT GLENEAGLE/ ARE PERFECT NOW

The 13th Green at Gleneagles

PLAY THE HI/TORIC /COTCH COUR/E/ THI/ /UMMER

Plan now to enjoy THE vacation you have been promising yourself since you first succumbed to the lure of the Ancient and Honorable. Think of teeing off in the land where bairns cut their teeth on niblicks and brassies, and the nineteenth hole still thrives — bonny Scotland, the gowfer's paradise!

Only that vast water hazard, the Atlantic, stretches between you and the land of your dreams—and that's easily played if you cross on a White Star, Red Star or Atlantic Transport liner. Great numbers of golf enthusiasts travel to Europe every summer on these luxurious ships. You will meet them on *yours* going over. They take the same pride in a superbly-appointed vessel that they do in a well-planned golf course. Instinctively they select the best among both.

In our fleets you have a choice of such famous liners as the *Majestic* (world's largest ship), *Olympic, Homeric, Belgenland, Lapland, Pennland, Arabic, Adriatic, Baltic, Cedric, Minnewaska, Minnetonka*, etc. —and two remarkable ships, the *Minnekahda* and *Minnesota*, that carry TOURIST Third Cabin passengers exclusively.

FREQUENT SAILINGS

WHITE /TAR LINE
RED /TAR LINE · ATLANTIC TRAN/PORT LINE
INTERNATIONAL MERCANTILE MARINE COMPANY
*For full information address No. 1 Broadway, New York,
our offices elsewhere or authorized steamship agents.*

*View from the
Gleneagles Hotel*

From a New York journal 1929

But there's an old adage that cakes can't be made without a bit of egg-breaking, and in the case of the Gleneagles Hotel (a very fruity and succulent 'cake' indeed) the Railway incurred the lasting wrath of their neighbours when naming their venture after the adjoining estate. Gleneagles, a wild and rocky terrain and once the haunt of the golden eagle, has been the family estate of the Haldanes of Gleneagles for 700 years. They've had a Gleneagles Castle somewhere in the middle of that terrain for about 500 of them. Back in 1911 the Caledonian Railway asked the family's permission to change the name of the local station from Crieff Junction to Gleneagles, and this was granted. But permission to use the name for the new hotel was neither sought nor given.

In 1928, with daily reports of the junketing taking place just a couple of miles from the family hearth, its owner wrote to the *Daily Record* in Glasgow:

I am well aware that, owing to the outrageous and uncalled-for-attempt made by the officials of the late Caledonian Railway Company and by what the LMS have thereby succeeded to, the public have been led to think the LMS company OWN Gleneagles.

Our family has owned Gleneagles since the 12th century, and you will appreciate that we very much resent being mixed up with a modern railway hotel . . . You lately published pictures in connection with the burial of Lord Haldane at my private chapel here, and certainly this was correctly described as at Gleneagles, but from your description of the opening of the new golf course, people might think that he was buried on the golf course, so you will see the absurdity of calling the golf course Gleneagles.

Mr. Matheson, who more than anyone else was responsible for the misuse of my name, wrote more than once to assure me that 'nothing was further from the minds of the company than to attempt to take the honoured name of Gleneagles', yet he actually had the audacity to mark the forks and spoons made for the railway hotel with the plain word 'Gleneagles' – not 'Hotel'.

Well, absurd and audacious though it may have been at the time, everything had gone too far for changes to be made and, to the best of my knowledge, the two Gleneagles establishments have gone their separate ways ever since, each carefully ignoring the other's existence.

As in the case of Blairgowrie, James Braid was invited up from Walton Heath to lay out the original King's and Queen's courses at Gleneagles, three years after he won the last of his five Opens in 1910. There have been some changes since, but few who have trodden the courses or watched TV Celebrity Golf being played there would find it easy to accept that they were carved from a 'virgin wilderness of gorse and heather with picks, shovels, and horse-drawn carts'. Braid was responsible for many great courses but always considered Gleneagles his greatest achievement.

There is no record of how long he spent personally on designing King's and Queen's, or what his charges were for so doing, but it's a fairly safe bet he didn't get the train back to Walton Heath on the day he arrived; and the bottom line on his bill was probably a little over the £10 he charged Blairgowrie for consultation on their Rosemount course 20 years later.

In 1928 a third course was designed by the head greenkeeper as a nine-holer, and this was named Prince's when extended to 18 holes in 1974. A fourth 18-hole course, the Glendavon, was opened in 1980.

All four courses are beautiful to walk, play or survey with greens, bunkers, water and woodland immaculately sculpted against a backdrop of scenic beauty. But then everybody has heard Peter Alliss and his colleagues enthusing about their surroundings during the early Celebrity Golf features run by the BBC at Gleneagles. There is little doubt about the popularity of the event among golfers and non-golfers alike, even if the quantity and quality of Waterford crystal lavished on the showbiz personalities involved may have seemed a bit over the top – as all too often neither their golf nor charisma was of a show-stopping nature. In fact, the *Gleneagles Souvenir Book*, published by Joint Marketing and Publishing Services Ltd of London W11, provided an interesting behind-the-scenes history to the event, some of which they have allowed to be used for what follows.

The BBC wanted something to extend the appeal of golf for family-viewing, instead of just presenting contests between the experts. So, to play in turn with experts Tom Weiskopf and Peter Oosterhuis, they put together entertainers Christopher Lee, Jimmy Tarbuck, Ronnie Corbett, and one or two others, including Fred MacMurray from Hollywood, and sent them up to Turnberry for a week in 1974 with the intention of filming ten matches. Each to consist of Tom and an entertainer of little-known golfing ability playing Peter with another man of the same ilk. But that first year only seven matches were filmed in the course of a week as it never stopped blowing a force-ten gale, with rain lashing down diagonally every day.

Nobody knew if it would catch on, but when the opinion polls calculated that four million people watched it on BBC five months later, plans were put in hand to do it again the following year. Only in the hope of finding better weather they shifted the action from tempestuous Turnberry to the more sheltered Gleneagles. This time Bing Crosby and

Howard Keel were the imported stars, and among the home-produced variety were Dickie Henderson and Charlie Drake. When the BBC received complaints over the scarecrow-like dress of one of them (James Hunt, the racing driver) they apologised and claimed they couldn't really lay down standards as the big names weren't getting paid. [Just having all found while playing golf all week at Gleneagles!]

In 1976 the professionals were Johnny Miller and Tony Jacklin, with Sean Connery, Burt Lancaster, Val Doonican, and a much better-dressed racing-driver this time – Jackie Stewart – among the stars.

'The amazing thing,' said a BBC producer, 'you had these people who were so used to facing millions on stage and TV, and capable of hitting a ball up to 250 yards on the practice fairway, but the moment a TV camera focused on them for the start of their golf match of the week they'd crack up.' It was quite an insight to learn how nervous some of them could be. George C. Scott, who played the part of 'blood-and-guts' General Patton in the film was also invited in 1976. He booked into the hotel at Gleneagles on arrival and booked out again the following morning. Nobody saw the going of him and nobody ever learned why. [It was probably for similar reasons given by King George V when tossing his clubs up in the loft – as described in Chapter 4.]

Almost without exception the celebrities were nervous and stressed at the thought of playing golf against top professionals at the game. People who were cool and calm on stage or screen were like you or me on the tee with a top golfer. And the stress was still very much in evidence long after the game was over.

But Fred MacMurray, though desperately ill with cancer and after a round in the most awful weather, came in at the end of it and – with his wife June Haver at the piano – contributed towards one of the greatest evenings of impromptu entertainment known in the series. The book said, however, that it was something of an exception. The American celebrities were usually far more introverted than their British counterparts. After all even Sean Connery had been known to joke – unless he lost!

As the series continued the field broadened: Colin Cowdrey, Geoff Lewis, Lew Hoad, Mark Thatcher, Jack Lemmon, Douglas Bader, are just a few of the celebrated names mentioned. The professionals changed too and, when Lee Trevino was installed, the programme achieved an even higher popularity rating.

A natural jester, a bon viveur, the life and soul of a party, are some of the popular opinions of Lee Trevino. (A man who is quoted as saying that he holds a one-iron over his head if caught on the course in an electric storm. Not even God, he explains, can hit a one-iron!) But the book says that few would reconcile this with his actual life-style when participating in the action at Gleneagles. When his game finished he'd return to the hotel, have one beer with his playing pals as a show of sociability, and then make for his room. He'd have his dinner sent up and stay there, watching television, until he retired – early. He had a daily supply of ice-cream sent over from Glasgow and entertained the supplier to dinner once during the week. Except for the final night, that's all anybody in the hotel ever saw of the fun-loving, wise-cracking Lee Trevino. On the other hand you can't blame him for wanting to avoid the bustling throng and banal attempts to intrude on his wind-down period after a day's work on the course.

Some of the celebrities, said Peter Alliss in his autobiography, still took liberties with the lavish hospitality ladled out to them, like Mars Bars and tee pegs – not to mention bottles of Dom Perignon – charged to their room, and in turn to the BBC. He doesn't name the culprits, but looking through the list of invitees over the years and marking off which names one thought were guilty of which acts of pettiness would be an absorbing fireside game for the long winter evenings. Something like Trivial Pursuits. Only I doubt if Peter would risk providing a list of correct answers to see who got it right.

Putting history to one side again and reverting to my arrival at this latter-day self-indulgence hostel, the reception area of the Gleneagles hotel continued to bustle with the arrival of new car-loads and yet another coach-load of pleasure seekers. So I went walkabout, taking in the features of the place: elegant shops, ritzy restaurants, American Bar. It must be the psychological effect of the name because, whereas I wouldn't short-list dry martinis among my everyday bar-side habits, entering an American one sets up a gastric urge for their national drink: very dry, very cold, stirred but not shaken, and straight-up with a couple of green olives, transfixed on a cocktail stick, resting on the rim of the glass.

While waiting for Ian Wilson, the hotel marketing manager with whom I'd made a 12.30 pm appointment – and for my room to be ready – I lunched on three of them, each served a little drier and colder than the previous one, and soaked them up with a freshly-cut smoked salmon sandwich. Ian apologised for being a little after our appointed time, but was told that waiting around in the ambiance of his hotel while indulging in the quality of its martinis was a privilege. He preferred a gin and tonic himself.

He explained that the hotel bookshop operated on an independent franchise arrangement and made its own decisions on what books to stock, but to let him know how I'd got on with its manager when we met again in the bar for a noggin after he'd finished his afternoon stint in the office.

Before calling on the bookshop I strolled over to see Ian Marchbanks, golf professional at Gleneagles for the past 30 years, in his well-stocked shop, who explained the long-standing arrangement he had with the hotel bookshop: he wouldn't stock golf books if they didn't sell golf-clubs, golf-umbrellas, or golf-shoes. It worked too. Nevertheless, having seen the book sent to Ian Wilson, he complimented me on it and bought a signed copy for himself. I reciprocated by buying a ball-wiping towel and half-a-dozen balls emblazoned with the Gleneagles crest, spending just a little more with him than he had with me.

Back at the bookshop they took three copies to sell, and I bought from them a copy of *Today's Golfer,* as the Secretary at Blairgowrie had mentioned seeing a double-page spread of one chapter from *If it wasn't for Golf . . . !* in the May publication. Back in my room – yes, the desk clerk brought the key for room 338 while I was on my third martini – little time was wasted in phoning editor Bill Robertson to tell him what a grand job he'd made of its presentation – as already explained in the Prologue.

When Ian Wilson learned (over our next meeting in the bar) that I was to write something for *Today's Golfer* in which opinions of Gleneagles might be included, he wasted little time in providing yet more glossy literature on the ever-increasing number of luxuries and leisure activities visitors to Gleneagles could expect. But as the object of this book is to entertain and inform from a golfing point of view, those needing to know more about the quality of riding, shooting, fishing, rock-climbing, walking, or even ballooning (with either one or two 'l's') need but phone the hotel and keep toes well clear of the letter box when the Gleneagles Marketing Pack crashes through the flap next morning!

One thing that's difficult to forget is what Gleneagles did to my golf game for the rest of 1989.

After Ian Wilson went home I got my clubs from the car for a leisurely knock around the nine-hole pitch-and-putt course. That's all there was going to be time for before the light failed. And very pleasant it was too, clonking a couple of balls off each tee with a 9-iron or pitching wedge. Until, when about half-way round, an exceptionally laid-back effort had the ball flying low at about 45 degrees off line in the direction of silly mid-off. Then came a similar shot – and soon after that yet another. Until, pent with fear and frustration, I knew only too well where the next one would go before even starting the backswing. Another bout of the dreaded 'shanks' had infiltrated and infected the Morley golfing machine, and six months of swing- and confidence-rebuilding would have to take place before I could get back to a blithe and carefree round with healthy people again.

Only chronic 'shankers' – of which I'm one – will recognise the symptoms and depression that comes with an attack, and the iron was etched deep in my soul when wending wearily back to room 338 after dumping the wretched bag back in the boot.

But it's surprising what a shower, change of clothes, and a couple of martinis back in the bar can do for a shattered morale, even though it was the earlier intake of those 'stirred-but-not-shaken' concoctions that had brought about the casual approach and that first floppy-wristed error. After that it's all in the mind; and the greater the apprehension and over-correction the more devastating the whole wretched thing becomes.

Chatting in the bar with a couple of Americans from the mid-West (one of whom was not long over an attack himself) they kindly suggested that I share their table for dinner as they thought I'd only brood if dining alone. There was certainly no brooding around that table over the next couple of hours in the magnificence of the Strathearn Restaurant, and although any one of our individual bills (we each signed our own, with wine, etc., at the table equally split three ways) could have fed all three of us comfortably in a Berni Inn, I knew just how those early Gleneagles bon-viveurs must have been enchanted by it all 60 years ago. (Don't remember any 'pyjama cigarettes', though; but being neither a smoker nor a pyjama-packer I didn't miss anything!)

The next day started with a 7.15 swim in the heated pool over in the Country Club Annexe, but the water was far too warm for my particular liking. Then I noticed a couple of guests out in the sharp morning air, clad only in swimming trunks, gingerly lowering themselves into large steaming barrels recessed end-on into a paved rock garden close by the Annexe. So I went out and did likewise. It was a matter of squatting eyeball-to-eyeball opposite another bather while hot water jetted and bubbled away around all your vital parts below the rim of the tub and the morning breeze blew straight off the Grampians on to that portion of your head and shoulders projecting above it – while all the time exchanging polite conversation about golf, climate, family life, and the whereabouts of Halley's Comet between sightings. Very exhilarating and friendly. Exposing the wet and well-warmed portion of the Morley anatomy to that chilly Grampian zephyr when clambering out made the over-heated pool more than welcome when I scurried back through the glass doors of its enclosure.

Prestigious national and international money-spinning golf competitions are the ambition of many Clubs, but these events are denied to most because of difficulty in conforming with what the organisers expect the venue to provide. This is especially so when big names are known to be coming under starter's orders and big crowds are expected. Some of the most recurrent snags include insufficient hotel accommodation in the area – as in the case of Carnoustie; or insufficient spectator facilities – as with Prestwick; or, generally, lack of suitable space for the vast tented city of shops, bars, restaurants, and hospitality suites that are a feature of most outdoor sporting events today. But Gleneagles has all of these – in spades – plus charisma far in excess of that possessed by many of the long-established venues for the top competitions.

The only fly in the ointment as far as the decision-makers were concerned was that it hadn't a golf course considered to be a stiff enough challenge to the big-hitting, pin-splitting, human golfing machines of today. So Gleneagles was in the process of 'baking another cake' – in the shape of a soul-destroying championship course – with Jack Nicklaus himself as the 'master baker'. But two 'eggs' had to be broken into the 'mix' – the Glendavon and Prince's courses, both of which were closed and 'cannibalised' for the desired end-product.

The new venture is planned for completion in 1992, and with the incentives and amenities its current owners – the muscular Guinness conglomerate – can bring to bear, there's little doubt that the Gleneagles cash-registers will be running hotter than ever once the new course opens.

After checking out, and while having a final word with Ian Wilson, I was asked by John-the-Greeter if he should bring the car over for my luggage. Ian had phoned earlier from his home to say he'd like to see me if possible before I left. His purpose was to provide a copy of the handsome *Gleneagles Souvenir Book* mentioned earlier. If and when he ever reads this chapter he'll see his gift was put to good use.

Belatedly remembering that for John to move my car after it had been out all night was courting trouble, I hurried across to where it was parked but could smell the flooded carburettors even before the forlorn beat of the whirring starter motor hit my ears. Poor old John couldn't be blamed for not knowing that the automatic choking system had failed a few months earlier and that the car now had a manual choke, with its operating knob hidden in a corner of the dashboard. Taking over the controls I yanked out the choke knob impatiently; and the whole 'shooting-match' finished up in my lap as the welded Bowden-wire joint at the carburettor end came apart.

There was no way of getting the thing hooked up again in the car-parking area of Gleneagles – it needed proper repair-shop facilities. John suggested a phone call to one in Auchterarder, about 2 miles away, to ask for a mechanic to be sent up. But with little time for that sort of thing I had him help me fiddle around until, with careful coaxing, the engine spluttered into life and eventually settled down to fire steadily on all cylinders.

Having shown appreciation to the good man in time-honoured fashion I drove away, with the choke-knob assembly and two feet of wire lying useless on the seat beside me. Sight of tractors on the golf course and other mechanical equipment working about the place brought the thought that there must surely be skilled fitters working within the Gleneagles complex to keep it all up to scratch. And with so much of the business they were after dependent on people travelling long distances by motor car, an offer of emergency service operating from a fully-equipped repair shop within the Gleneagles complex and easily reached on foot, or via the main switchboard, might well be worth featuring among the glossy literature of a marketing pack. It would certainly appeal more to a frustrated motorist if the needs arose than the offer to phone and ask for a mechanic to come up from an Auchterarder garage.

Over to you Mr Wilson!

Gleneagles was another of the 1989 venues revisited when I went up for the Scottish 'hickories' in May 1990. Ian Wilson had been promoted within the Group and Ann Parker was now the Hotel marketing manager. On reading through some of my draft with a view to bringing it up to date, she came to the bit about the hot tubs and told of spending her honeymoon at Gleneagles some years before going to work there, when the two newlyweds 'hot-tubbed' together in a blinding snowstorm!

Construction of the 'macho' Championship Course was proceeding to plan and only that week was it decided to call it 'The Monarch's'. They had by this time also opened a nine-holer, named 'The Wee Course', as was the original one laid out by their head greenkeeper – until that was renamed 'The Prince's' when extended to 18 holes in 1934.

The Country Club Annexe had been enlarged and now incorporated a Champney's Health Spa, similar to the one at Tring near Aylesbury, which also happens to be part of the Guinness Group.

The place was teeming with overseas visitors, as usual, when I drove off with a cheery wave to the kilted 'John-the-Greeter', still doing his stuff at the main entrance. He waved back – without recognition of course – and there wasn't time to stop and ask how many car-starting problems he'd encountered since we last met.

To close the chapter we need to return to my 8am departure from Gleneagles on Thursday 27 April 1989.

—— 13 ——

Troon

Once on the main highway and heading in the general direction of my 11.30 appointment 100 miles away with Franco Galgani, general manager of the Marine Highland Hotel, Troon, signals started arriving from the 'engine-room' that I'd started without breakfast. It was deliberate self-denial, as calorie intake since arriving in Scotland had been well over the top. But there was no sense in overdoing the masochism and with the distance yet to be covered that morning a stop for some sustenance made sense.

But familiar road-signs indicating when Services were to be had at the next junction proved a myth. Twice I turned off at one of these landmarks only to find another lesser road leading off into the distance with no feeding or fuelling facilities anywhere in sight. Not wanting to wander half-way across Scotland in the wrong direction in search of a cup of coffee, I'd abandon the search each time and claw my way back to the road just left hoping something more in my favour would soon show up.

Third time proved lucky, somewhere around Cumbernauld, where they did a nice line in black coffee and thin buttered toast. I had quite a mind-over-matter tussle resisting full-house breakfast within sight and smell of the counter when ordering, but sitting nibbling toast and sipping coffee at a table furthest away from temptation and with my back to it all while studying a road map, helped to shut out haunting visions of sausages, bacon and eggs – with or without the mushrooms!

The road map was needed to find the best route for clearing the southern suburbs of Glasgow, as traffic generated by Scotland's busiest city would be a lot heavier than anything encountered so far. The one selected proved a sound choice as the worst was avoided by heading well south on the M74, before striking west on the A71. This took me to Kilmarnock, and finally Troon.

The Marine Highland Hotel, with its 72 luxury bedrooms and three restaurants, looks out over the Royal Troon Golf Course and the Firth of Clyde beyond it. Just a narrow footpath separates the fairway of the 18th hole from the hotel frontage. As the Club was to host the Open Championship about ten weeks hence, contractors were already at work erecting scaffolding for spectator stands around the course.

Franco Galgani said his hotel was fully booked at the moment and would remain that way until long after the tumult and shouting of the big July event had died down, but for all the people around at that moment we could just as well have been aboard the *Marie Celeste*! He explained that most hotel guests were out playing their heart out round the arena where the world's greatest were due to perform in a couple of months, so that when the time came to watch it on TV they could boast to all and sundry of the miraculous 40-footer they'd sunk on the hole that Faldo or Trevino was just seen to three-putt. In another couple of weeks the course would be closed to allow a bit more meanness to be grown into it before the giants came to tear it apart.

Franco had enjoyed the complimentary book I'd sent and, bringing it out for personalising, ordered 24 to display and sell at his Reception desk; believing that his visitors might well be glad of some light reading between the trials and tribulations to be encountered outside.

Troon Golf Club was formed in 1878 by the gentry living in and around the town. It was given Royal status on reaching its centenary in 1978, and has hosted six Open Championships to date. Finding highlights in its history to include here was proving difficult until Laurence Viney, golf historian *par excellence* and past-editor of *The Golfer's Handbook*, kindly lent me *Troon Golf Club – Its History from 1878*, compiled by Ian M. Mackintosh and published by the Club in 1974. I don't know why they didn't wait four more years and celebrate their centenary with it. There might then have been some reference to their titular transition from Old Troon to Royal Troon. As it is they still have nothing very historical about being granted the Royal Charter in 1978, other than a framed certificate on the Clubhouse wall.

Before speaking to Laurence I phoned the Secretary at Troon and was told that as they no longer had a copy of their history they would send the Club's current *Handbook* , but with the help of Laurence's volume I wrote this chapter over Easter 1990. When the *Handbook* arrived a couple of days later I anticipated having to up-date my typescript, but no changes were necessary other than the insertion of this paragraph. The *Handbook* proved to be two years older than the 1974 book used for my research!

Like so many others of its ilk, the Club history book wasn't half as suspense-packed as, say, *The Day of the Jackal*, but leaving the geography and geology of the course to one side – not to mention the genealogy of Club rank and file – the ensuing potted highlights of its past 112 years should make interesting reading.

Unlike the east coast courses, there is no record of knockabout golf being played beside the sea at Troon before anybody deciding to put a Golf Club together. Some of the townsfolk maintained, however, that citizens of Troon had ancient rights to the common land that had been leased to the Club. It could never be proved and was therefore rejected when the subject of a legal report in 1934.

It was William Arthur John Cavendish, 6th Duke of Portland who, through his agent, Fred Turner of Kilmarnock, agreed to let off some of his land on a yearly rental basis for the local gentry to build themselves a golf course. A meeting was called and held in the Portland Arms, Troon, on Saturday 16 March 1878, when a Captain and a Secretary/Treasurer were appointed, together with a working committee. The latter were entrusted with getting the course built, and the 'Links Custodian' from nearby Prestwick Golf club was invited over to tell them how to do it.

In March 1879 a total of 58 members attended the first AGM in the 'clubhouse' (a stripped-down railway carriage) to which the luxury of a lavatory was added in 1880. The Duke himself became an honorary member that year, but there's no mention whether the presence of the one influenced that of the other!

In 1881 the Committee decided that golf in Troon was now important enough to introduce a handicapping system. At that time there were just 6 holes hacked out of some pretty rough ground, but by 1883 there were 12. Then they 'went for gold' when with the help of their first professional, George Strath, the course was extended to 18 holes. In the absence of today's sophisticated mowing equipment, Mrs Briggs, tenant of the local farm, was engaged to graze 300 sheep on the outlying holes!

Nobody wanted to spend too much on the project as the Club only had a yearly tenancy from the Duke in those days but when more ground was negotiated further inland, for the building of a 'Relief Course' to cater for flooding problems at the Old, a 20-year lease was granted at a yearly rent of £85 for the two courses.

Ladies are still not allowed to play on the Championship Course at Troon unless competing in a major national or international competition. Neither can they enter the Member's Clubhouse unless for lunch or dinner when the guest of a member. But they had their own Ladies Golf Club as early as 1882. When instituted they chose for their motto, 'Quo rectius eo melius' which, we are told, means 'The straighter the better'. Few will disagree with that one – whatever the context.

At first they were allowed to use the Old Course on a grace and favour basis, despite no shortage of objection from the more misogynic members. A compromise was reached when a few holes were created for them in the north-west corner of the links, and a crude shed for a Clubhouse provided; whereby Troon Ladies Golf Club was a self-contained unit very soon after its origination. The men, being only too pleased to manage and maintain things for them just as long as it kept females from the male strongholds, built their ladies a nice new two-storey Clubhouse in 1897. Two years earlier they'd been given permission to play on the new Relief Course.

Back in the early days local tradespeople and artisans claimed the right to play over the Old Course. There was much feuding and fighting – mainly verbal, I believe – with the Club members, who strongly objected to the *hoi polloi* latching on to what they felt to be the private perks of the gentry. The Club made a point of having its professional on duty on the first tee each Saturday to put the block on anyone trying to play without the necessary credentials of membership.

But membership being a privilege granted only to the chosen few – as is the wont with most private clubs – and play being denied to others by those in control, the locals petitioned the Duke to intercede on their behalf. Being a kind old Duke, who probably preferred deferential tradespeople to self-seeking socialites – much as the Queen seems to prefer obsequious tribal chiefs to obstreperous party ones – he succeeded in bringing the necessary pressure to bear on the Club because the 42 petitioners, mainly clerks and shopkeepers, were given a restricted membership in 1894 for a subscription of ten shillings a year. They were issued with identity cards permitting limited playing rights as Troon residents, but were not allowed to play on certain high days, holidays, medal days, or Saturdays from April to August inclusive.

When the 'Relief Course' opened in 1895, the Portland Golf Club was created and those plebeian 'second-class' citizens of the Old Club were given new identity cards, saying they were members of Portland Golf Club, and confined to play only on the new Relief Course. Permission to play thereafter on the Old Course was withdrawn except by special dispensation of the Old Troon committee. And that, I understand, didn't come easily.

It wasn't until 1923 that Troon was first selected as a venue for the Open Championship – by now quite a prestigious event – due to Muirfield having to forego its turn while alterations to its course were taking place. It was the first time in the history of the event that professionals were allowed to use the hosting Clubhouse, thanks to protestations made by the charismatic Walter Hagen. James Braid once again comes into our story as, when called in to prepare the course for standards suitable for the occasion, he introduced about 40 new bunkers.

There was also much controversy at the eleventh hour over a question of illegal clubs. American and British professionals were arriving with holes punched in the face of their clubs to improve the stopping and backspin effects of their shots. Two days before the event started the R&A ruled that punched clubs were illegal. As a result Troon's professional staff worked day and night on the competitors' clubs with all the filing tools they could beg, borrow, or steal from surrounding workshops and shipyards.

Arthur Havers won the Open that year, pipping runner-up Walter Hagen (who won it the previous year at Sandwich – where he promptly presented the £100 cheque to his caddy – and the following one at Hoylake) by sinking his bunker shot at the 18th. There were 222 entries, and it took 295 shots over 72 holes to win Arthur his first prize of £100.

Twenty-seven years were to pass before the Open next came to Troon in 1950, when Bobby Locke beat 262 competitors with a 279, the first sub-280 score since they started playing the Competition over 72 holes 60 years earlier. He got £300 prize money for that.

Then in 1962 Arnold Palmer won it at Troon with a record score of 276 against an all-time high of 379 entries, receiving £1,400 for his trouble; while in 1973 Tom Weiskopf hit the jackpot of £5,500 with another 276 against a new record of 569 entries. That was the year one competitor took 15 strokes to play the 126-yard 8th – the Postage Stamp – the shortest hole on the Championship circuit. The same year and at the same hole TV viewers saw Gene Sarazen hole out in one!

In 1982 Troon, now Royal Troon, again hosted the Open, with Tom Watson coming home in front of no fewer than 1,121 entries, to pick up £32,000 for a score of 284; and in July 1989 Mark Calcavecchia received £80,000 for beating 1,482 others with a four-round aggregate of 275. It was in 1962 – Palmer's year – that a lady professional first entered for the Open. She was a Mrs Beck, from Wentworth. The R&A didn't go much on the idea and turned her down. They have no record of similar applications from the gentler sex since then.

In the same year there was a story of five American couples, unknown to each other but all on honeymoon, attending the Open at Troon and agreeing they'd meet again at Troon 11 years later for the 1973 event. Four of the men did – but alone, each having gone through the divorce courts by this time. The fifth pair of honeymooners were both there for the reunion, and credited their continuing wedded bliss to the fact that he didn't play golf!

It was the 6th Duke of Portland again who, 16 years after the formation of Troon Golf Club in 1878, laid the foundation stone for the Marine Highland Hotel to be built on its perimeter. The same noble lord performed the opening ceremony in April 1897. The cost of the project finished up in the vicinity of £90,000 – quite a lot of money for a resort hotel in those days, but it is still the largest and most prestigious in town. As already said, its frontage runs parallel to the 18th fairway; about as close to it as the frontage of the Old Course Hotel is to the Fairway of 'my old friend' – the 17th at St Andrews!

There's the story I read somewhere about that great amateur golfer and fellow-left-hander, 'Laddie' Lucas, who had a tendency to spray his tee shots more than somewhat – especially after a particularly festive evening. On this occasion his opening drive from the 1st tee on the Old Course at Troon sailed into the Marine Highland Hotel, but too many good stories like this are woefully short on essential detail – so I can't say whether it went through the front door, dining room window, or into one of the first floor bedrooms. Nor whether it smashed a bottle of beer, glass of champers, plate of porridge, or some lady's teeth in a glass by the side of her bed.

I know I could say it did any of these things, but that would be gilding the facts – thereby jeopardising the future of this book as a quotable reference work on golfing history. But there's nothing to stop a reader embellishing it as he thinks with a couple of the foregoing – adding the rider that he knows it's true because he read it in Sam Morley's *By Yon Bonnie Links!* but can't remember whether it was the porridge or the teeth!

When reading through the finished typescript I phoned 'Laddie' Lucas to see if he could expound further on the story, having found his address and phone number among his history and achievements in *Who's Who*.

After listening to a scintillating series of anecdotes from his book *The Sport of Princes* (published in 1980 by Stanley Paul and in which the foregoing appears) I was treated to another 'out-of-bounds' story relating to the time when, as a wartime Spitfire pilot, he was shot up by a Messerschmitt 109 after a raid on enemy-occupied France and was trying to get home on a defunct engine. Rather than bale out and chance being found and picked up from the chilly Channel he decided to try making his home golf course, Prince's, in a long easy glide.

Aiming his silent Spitfire at the long 1st he missed the fairway, missed the 6th, missed the 8th, and finished 'out of bounds' in the rushes at the back of the old 9th green! And Prince's was home, literally. His father built the course at the turn of the century; the family lived in a big house adjoining the clubhouse; and he reckoned that falling from his nursery window when but a babe in 1915 would have put him on the first tee!

But due to proximity of the enemy and defence regulations, golf was not played there in either of the Great Wars. During

World War One in fact, some of the greens were used for mortar-fire target practice. By our own side, that is, not the opposition! (Judging by some of the awful things done to some of out loveliest courses, I'd say Whitehall in wartime was more anti-Golf than anti-German!)

Putting his wartime and political career to one side (Wing Commander at HQ Air Defence 1944 and MP for Brentford-and-Chiswick 1950 to 1959) his golfing achievements alone merit Hall of Fame mention. But as this is a Scottish-orientated book, I'll just say he played in the Walker Cup in 1936, 1947 and 1949 (Captain on the last occasion) and also provided another tale of his because that, too, relates to one of the famous courses featured elsewhere in this volume.

Apparently he was lying 7th and leading Lawson Little by one stroke for the low-amateur prize, after three rounds in the 1935 Open Championship at Muirfield. Confident that even a modest 72 would make him leading Brit., and just a little better might even bring 'best-amateur' victory over his American opponent, he indulged himself freely over lunch before going out for the final round.

Unwrapping his ball on the first tee (yes, they used to be hermetically sealed in crinkly paper in those happy days) he saw Henry Longhurst hurrying towards him – they were also the days when Henry was better built for hurrying – clutching a telegram addressed to Laddie. It had not long arrived and told him, baldly, that he'd achieved a third-class in his Tripos exam at Cambridge – which just enabled him to continue his dream of playing University golf for the ensuing two years.

This sobering thought, coupled with that euphoric lunch, helped him go out and shoot 81 in that fourth round at Muirfield! (Even so, he was still the leading British amateur!)

Like Gleneagles Hotel, and some of the other top class watering holes featured in these pages, the Marine Highland Hotel is anxious for accolades as a leisure complex catering for every amenity sought by the discerning visitor to Troon, and not just as a convenient 'dormy-house' for touring golfers renowned for their indifference to the more aesthetic things in life. It was not until some time after digesting the Old Troon history book and reading between some of its lines, that I realised why Colin Baird, my Strathclyde sales agent and a young man of Troon, seemed a little ill-at-ease when awaiting my arrival for our initial meeting at the Marine Highland Hotel. He played his golf on the Municipal Park, a grand complex of three 18-hole courses – The Darley, Loch Green, and Fullerton – of which Loch Green, the toughest and a pure links course, is often used for qualifying rounds in the Open.

Membership of Royal Troon is drawn from the privileged hierarchy throughout the West of Scotland and is comparable in its élitist image to Muirfield. With the result that it hasn't much in common with the true 'Troonian'. Waiting for me in its proximity was not much to the liking of my young friend, even though he was currently Vice-Captain of St Meddans Golf Club, one of the clubs that shared the golfing facilities of Loch Green and Darley with similar clubs to their own, and the general public.

Nevertheless Royal Troon was to give him one of the biggest thrills of his life when, ten weeks after we met, he caddied in the Open for Robert Karlsson, the only Swedish player to complete the tournament, and drawn to play with Seve Ballesteros in the final round. In 1988, Colin had taken himself down to Lytham St Annes in search of a 'bag' in the Open and caddied for Christian Harden, the British Amateur Champion who, unfortunately, didn't make the half-way cut.

Colin and his younger brother, Alan, each with a BSc, had started their own business in 1988. Called *Pro-Guide*, it involves surveying existing golf courses and, from their measurements and drawings, preparing those attractive hole-by-hole identification and distance charts that so many serious golfers like to pull from their hip pocket and study carefully before selecting a club and direction that'll put the ball 4 feet from the pin. Only all too often indifferent selection and ability puts it 40 yards left, right, short, or over! He tells me that *Pro-Guide* has done charts for about ten courses so far and, when I phoned him on a couple of points in this chapter, he said they'd landed a contract to produce 15 for the Scottish PGA tournaments in 1990.

His great-uncle, Bill Milligan, is an old friend and ex-neighbour now living in Ayrshire and featured at length later in the book. When Colin was shown a copy of *If it wasn't for Golf . . . !* by great-uncle Bill he got in touch to ask if (a) I'd like to advertise in the next *Pro-Guide* he planned to produce (I believe he does an initial print run of a thousand for the professional of the course in question to sell in his shop) and (b) did I need an agent in his area? The answer to both was yes. But his *Pro-Guide* business now takes up all his time and my book sales in Scotland are handled by a full-time representative.

Leaving the Marine Highland Hotel, we visited his Clubhouse at Loch Green for a drink and some lunch. During which he showed me the Walter-Hagen-driver and told of a Competition they play there every year – ever since the great man himself presented them with his own favourite No.1 wood in 1923, in appreciation of the practice facilities provided by Loch Green when he played at Old Troon in the Open. It was proudly mounted on an Honours Board in the Clubhouse, with the names of the competition winner each year since 1924 engraved beneath it, but in June

1990 was generously donated to the newly-built St Andrews Museum of Golf described in Chapter 7.

At motor repair workshops next door to the Pro-Guide offices, the mechanics happened to be friends of the Baird brothers. Discussing chokes with them, they promised to have a replacement unit ready to fit in position by the time I was back from the next appointment at Bridge of Weir, near Paisley. Although every day had been warm and sunny so far, the nights had been equally cold and frosty. Without using plenty of choke next morning after the old chariot had been out on its own all night, there would certainly have been starting problems. Now, if things went to plan, there was every reason to hope there wouldn't be any.

14

Ranfurly Castle

With Colin Baird as companion and map-reader to help navigate the winding cross-country roads ahead, I was now en route to my third 100-year-old Club.

The visit involved a tiring and almost-abortive 75-mile round trip to Bridge of Weir, on the Strathgryfe Moors and about 6 miles west of Paisley. The roads bordering Ranfurly Castle Golf Club were well urbanised with large expensive-looking houses all around. Although about 15 miles west of the City centre, Bridge of Weir was generally recognised as a residential belt for Glasgow stockbrokers and their ilk.

Were this book aimed at a nomadic addict for use as a conventional golfing guide, there would have been no difficulty in filling a few pages with information gleaned from the Club's centenary booklet – riveting stuff, but more suited to one of Colin Baird's *Pro-Guides* than a four-colour souvenir of a noble Golf Club's centenary.

Each of the 18 holes was described in detail, and each had a name as well as a number. Some were simple and descriptive, like 'Westward Ho!' or 'Windy Ridge' – others a bit twee and Rob Roy-ish – like 'Pechin Brae' or 'Wee De'il'. But I couldn't see anyone wanting to read much further if this chapter had gone on in that vein.

Unlike most of the other places visited, there was nothing to be read about Ranfurly Castle Golf Club on the bookshelves of my collector friends; or in the libraries. The only historical records were in that souvenir booklet and most of those I considered too parochial to be included here.

Neither did anything newsworthy arise from my meeting with Mrs Thelma Gemmell, Club Secretary for the past eight years. She was awaiting my arrival to get a signature on the book I'd sent her, said she'd starting reading it, offered us a choice of tea or coffee, but just as soon as I was ready to leave she, too, had plans to be on her way for a fortnight's holiday in the Wye Valley.

The three-storey Clubhouse was spacious, beautifully panelled, highly burnished from top to bottom – and empty. Designed by one of Scotland's leading architects at the turn of the century, John Archibald Campbell, there was much rejoicing and celebration when it opened in 1905 but, except for the Secretary, the place was devoid of humanity 84 years later when Colin Baird and I saw it for the first time. Not for any dramatic reason – just that everybody was either out on the course, at business, or at home.

Asking about the history of the Club, I was given the colourful A4 brochure referred to earlier on the forthcoming centenary celebrations. Colin took the opportunity to describe the *Pro-Guide* services he could offer, and on the way out we stopped to admire the large paved patio at the back with its splendid outlook across the course and rolling landscape beyond. But there was a long tiring journey ahead and reaching Troon in time to get my car fixed took precedence over a rhapsodic survey of the local scenery.

And that's where the Ranfurly Castle Club saga almost ended.

A year later, when looking over what was to be the shortest chapter, I phoned Thelma Gemmell to ask if anything worth chronicling happened during the centenary year as I'd have liked to fatten up their involvement in this story. 'Well, yes', she said after thinking it over a bit, 'We did publish a very nice 140-page hardback book on the Club history at the end of it.' 'That's great news!', I told her, 'If you can send me a copy now I promise to send you one of *By Yon Bonnie Links!* soon after publication come the autumn. 'That sounds fair', she said, and acted on it. *Ranfurly Castle Golf Club – A Centenary History*, by Robert Crampsey, arrived a few days later with the compliments of the Committee. It proved one of the most enjoyable books of its kind I've yet read, with the author showing much wit and panache in presenting colourful highlights of what is all too often an unimaginative catalogue of long-forgotten people and events.

His book opens with the claim that Ranfurly Castle Golf Club must be unique in having elected its first and youngest-ever Life Member on its Foundation Day. The decision to form the Club was made in the Ranfurly Castle Hotel on the evening of Saturday 3 August 1889. During the meeting the newly-elected Captain, a Dr Mudie, was suddenly called away to attend a confinement. An important one as the mother-to-be was the wife of the newly-elected Chairman. On the Captain's return he announced the Chairman to be the father of a fine boy. Then came a proposal that the newborn babe be given Life Membership, whereby his birth would be linked with that of Ranfurly Castle Golf Club. There was no difficulty in finding a seconder, followed by a unanimous vote in favour.

A month before the start of World War Two, the Club received a congratulatory telegram on its Golden Jubilee from its first Life Member – now living in Canada – who happened to be celebrating his fiftieth birthday on the same day!

When that first meeting took place, Glasgow Golf Club and the Gailes Golf Club at Irvine, near Troon, were already over 100 years old. Other than those two there was not much else by way of Clubs in the West of Scotland. But with the development of the railway from Glasgow, Bridge of Weir saw possibilities of its growth as an up-and-coming inland spa and resort area for the more acceptable of the city's teeming hordes; and within a few weeks of that first meeting it was decided to lease enough land from their Vice-President, a local landowner, at £10 a year, for a nine-hole course to be laid out.

The first subscription was a guinea a year, with a £2 entrance fee. Sixty-two members were on the books when the course was officially opened on 2 November 1889 by the non-golfing President hitting first an air shot, and then a badly-topped one, off the first tee. But what he lacked in skill was well set off by his generous contributions to Club funds.

Hazards there were a-plenty in those early days and a local farmer was asked what he wanted in compensation to take his cattle off the course and only graze sheep!

The first professional-cum-greenkeeper, Willie Campbell from Prestwick, was paid £1 a week and helped design those first nine holes. He got an additional 6s.6d.a week for a storage-and-valet-service on members' clubs and clothes, and for a further tuppence a pair he also cleaned their boots.

In 1891 came a written complaint of a member cheating when winning a medal competition. He was accused of teeing up in the rough and of chucking his ball up on the green instead of hitting it there. But as the party in question happened to be the farmer with the rights to graze his cattle on the course, the Committee diplomatically did a 'sideways get-out' by punishing the miscreant's partner for putting the wrong score on the card!

Vandalism by those who objected to golf being played on the site was not unknown, and printed notices were posted around offering rewards for information leading to prosecution of the culprits.

A visitor who asked permission to play one Friday and Saturday and given it, was found to have played on Sunday when no play was ever allowed. He was barred from Ranfurly thereafter, although one of those responsible for banning him was seen to be having a bit of putting practice himself a few Sundays later. It took another 20 years and a long series of disputes before Sunday golf was at last voted in. Nevertheless a number of the more God-fearing members resigned in bitter protest.

The rough old shed that had done duty as a Clubhouse was so badly in need of repair that, when a new one was built at a cost of £300 in 1892, the old one was let for six months for a total sum of £5. Even then the lessee complained of what he would have to spend to make it usable, so they dropped the rent to £4 and said he could keep the lino, too, providing he took the shed 'as is'!

A woman was hired to keep the new Clubhouse clean, and one of her duties was to ensure that all coal buckets were left filled up each day.

By 1893 Willie Campbell, the professional, was reported as getting too big for his boots and seating himself with members in the Clubhouse. On being reprimanded he resigned and went elsewhere.

Ladies were now allowed to play before 5pm, except on Saturdays, holidays and match days. This would imply that the membership was largely a plebeian one, working weekdays and Saturday mornings in shop or office.

In 1895 the course was extended to 18 holes and

membership pegged at 400, after good response to advertisements in the Glasgow papers and men's clubs.

Troubles built up with the Ranfurly Castle Hotel, which was under contract to the Club as sole suppliers of refreshments. The minute book shows concern over their failure to provide Bass beer, a great favourite with the members; also over the hotel's objection to plans for a dormitory wing to the Clubhouse for Glasgow members to stay over on holidays or weekends. The hotel claimed it would be an infringement of their contract. So plans were put in hand to buy them out.

In 1903, 200 acres of farmland about half a mile from the station were bought for £6,500 and construction of the present golf course was started. Members were getting tired of sharing the one they rented with incontinent cattle, whose big feet crunched great holes in those parts of the course not already sullied with deposits.

To get money in from slow-paying members anybody in arrears was denied refreshments at the bar – on the grounds that to serve them would be in breach of the licensing laws. [I bet that worked!]

John Archibald Campbell, eminent Scottish architect, won a competition to construct a Clubhouse on the new site. It was formally opened in May 1905, when a tournament of top professionals was played on the course and in which Harry Vardon came third. Ten policemen were hired for crowd-control but there's no report of undue disturbance by forerunners of today's lager-louts in the new building or around the course.

When a member admitted to being drunk in the Clubhouse on a Sunday (nobody seemed to know how he happened to be there when everything was supposed to be closed down) another vote was taken on Sunday opening but the proposal was narrowly defeated. Then in 1910 the 'free-drinkers' tried again and, despite a petition against it signed by 600 locals, the seven-day golfers-and-'tipplers' finally got their way. But there were 35 resignations. The Captain (obviously of the 'No' brigade) complained that those responsible for loss of revenue from those 35 should hold themselves responsible for finding replacements to join the Club. That's if there were enough of the ungodly about prepared to seek membership of this latter-day Sodom and Gomorrah!

In 1915 a member who had his German nephew spending the summer at his home was accused by another of 'harbouring the enemy and being a pro-German traitor to his country!' The incensed member referred the insult to the Committee who sagely ruled it was a personal difference and refused to intervene. Law suits were threatened but wisdom prevailed as more serious matters took precedence.

Over 100 members were serving the country and excused subs. There were many casualties. There was also talk of ploughing up part of the course for growing crops, as the U-boats took their toll on our shipping. Crop-growing was forestalled by the Club allowing cattle to be grazed on the course, which meant fencing the greens and using 12" high flagsticks, as it was said the beasts were attracted to the greens by the long sticks. It was found the little ones, too, were just as attractive.

With so many men away ladies were allowed to play any time without a gentleman partner and, with the Ranfurly Castle Hotel now an Auxiliary Hospital, wounded servicemen were free to play, too.

Come the Armistice, things at the Club soon swung back to normal with a complaint that the directors had been tampering with the whisky. That too was settled amicably.

In 1923, master-golfer James Braid was called in to suggest improvements to the course, but when his proposals to alter the first and last two holes were put to a members' vote they were turned down. Obviously the master's word wasn't always the final one acted upon by those consulting him.

Objections to 'passive smoking' are not all that new. When a 'No Smoking' sign was put up in the dining room, a member took it down. When the steward put it up again the same member ripped it off the wall and tore it up in front of the steward. The Board had him make a full apology to the steward and provide a replacement at his own expense.

They were a kindly Committee at Ranfurly. When their professional confessed to pocketing green-fee takings in 1923 and investing the money in slow horses, he was dismissed. But it was just before Christmas and in answer to his pleas he was reinstated with a warning. Yet it wasn't long before he fell from grace again, received another caution, and finally shown the door within a year of that first offence.

A member won a prize designated to the value of £1.10s. He bought himself a pair of glass or china bowls for £2. 5s.6d. and sent the receipt to the Secretary with a request that the Club refund £1 10s. of it. The Secretary referred it to the R&A who said it wasn't on, as 'no money as part of a prize can be paid to an amateur'.

On 12 January 1924 a plaque was unveiled in the Clubhouse to the 22 of its members killed in the 1914–18 war.

In 1925, Protestant Churches of Scotland asked all Golf Clubs that opened on Sundays to stop doing so. Ranfurly Castle Golf Club decided to ignore them. It had taken so long to win the day and move with the times, they quite sensibly couldn't see the point in putting the clock back.

Society applications to play the course were granted to many bodies, such as the Glasgow Press Club, Scottish Shoe Trade, Glasgow Fruit Trade, and many other of the city establishments. But – shades of Edinburgh's Honourable Golfers – permission was refused to the Provincial Grand

Lodge of Freemasons of East Renfrewshire! Apparently they were 68 in number and more than the Club was prepared to allow.

With the Depression of the early 1930s membership shrank to 300, and economy was the order of the day both on the course and in the Clubhouse. In efforts to increase numbers and revenue, entrance fees and subs were reduced, ladies allowed in the Clubhouse at all times, the billiards table sold, and part of the land owned by the Club – but not the course itself – put on the market. Yet they were still generous employers, and when the greenkeeper died in hospital after an appendix operation – in those days long before social security and pension schemes – they continued to pay his full wages to his wife and six children for the ensuing six months before making more permanent arrangements to cater for the family's welfare.

Membership continued to fall and at the 280 level, in October 1934, it was decided to abolish entrance fees until numbers had risen above the 350 mark. They were soon reinstated as 84 joined in the next two months!

Came World War Two and a number of veterans of the previous conflict were recalled to the colours. Bridge of Weir was considered a safe area and there was talk of Glasgow children being evacuated and housed in the Clubhouse. The prospect of their genteel establishment being overrun by hordes of young hooligans from the Gorbals prompted a carefully-worded reminder to the Authorities on the perils of having children in any quantity on licensed premises. They never came.

The professional's shop was short of people to whom he could sell his stock and as scarcities grew it became even emptier when he could no longer find stock to sell. Despite sadly-depleted funds the Club compensated him in April 1941 with an ex-gratia payment of £26.

To forestall the risk of being told to plough up the course for agricultural purposes it was rented out for grazing sheep at £100 a year. They could well do with the cash.

With no petrol available for private motoring those few golfers travelling up from Glasgow would share a taxi. But their 'sweeties' they'd have to buy in town before setting out as with rationing and coupons 'sweeties' were no longer available from the Clubhouse.

With the West of Scotland Army HQ at Bridge of Weir, officers were allowed temporary membership for a three guinea subscription.

The Ministry of Agriculture finally ordered that the first and last two holes be put to the plough – more to conform with sacrifices demanded from other Clubs than the suitability of the soil to grow anything worthwhile. Nevertheless there are records of two crops of oats being harvested before the course was reinstated. After a bit of a struggle with Whitehall, the Club settled for £260 compensation once the war was over.

But while it still raged, golf balls, even old and battered ones were at a premium. Malaya was our main source of rubber, golf balls were made of rubber, and the Japs had Malaya. The Club pulled off quite an achievement in 1944 when it bought four dozen remoulds from the North British Rubber Company and sent them six dozen scruffy ones for a 'retread'.

In the absence of staff and stocks, meals and bar service were drastically restricted and members rationed to one glass of whisky or gin a week.

Subscriptions were pegged at four guineas for 1945, and with the end of the war concessions for temporary membership were withdrawn. Full membership was restricted to 320 with 70 places reserved for returning ex-servicemen; plus 150 ladies with 15 held for those coming back from the Forces.

Housing shortage was so acute that when a new greenkeeper was appointed he was allowed to live in the professional's workshop until a house could be found for him in the Bridge of Weir area.

The new man had the help of three German prisoners-of-war in reinstating the course, who were allowed to make their own way back to Johnstone Castle at the end of each day. One was said to have been sparring partner to Max Schmeling, the pre-war World Heavyweight Champion, but there's no record of anybody putting his claim to the test.

Shortages and rationing continued throughout Britain for a number of years after the war and Ranfurly Castle suffered with the rest. Liquor had to be bought on the black market and the bar couldn't help much – as it did of yore – towards the Club finances. White-coated waiters flitting about the verandah with laden trays were just nostalgic memories of the idyllic pre-war days.

Nevertheless efforts were made to return to a more gracious era by applying for clothing coupons whereby livery or uniforms could be made for the house staff; and stricter standards of dress and behaviour in the Clubhouse demanded when complaints were lodged that visitors wore their pullovers in the lounge and were known to buy drinks for the greenkeeper. So green fees were raised to 3s.6d. on weekdays and 7s.6d. on Saturdays in an effort to keep out undesirables.

The annual dinner-dance in Glasgow had to be cancelled in October 1947 because of restrictions on petrol, food, and liquor, but by the end of that year the whisky or gin ration in the Clubhouse had gone up to one small measure a day, with no restriction on rum – so things were looking up.

At the 1949 AGM subs for the following year were raised to six guineas, and three for ladies. The professional's retainer was to be £4 a week, and for that he was expected to keep the shop open every day, from Monday to Saturday, until 8.30pm.

In 1951 a Memorial Service was held for the five members of Ranfurly Castle Golf Club killed in the 1939–45 war.

After a disastrous fire in September 1946 had destroyed much of the roof, furniture and furnishings, rebuilding the Clubhouse was taking far longer than expected due to shortage of materials. Excuses about lack of hardwood for flooring were met with complaints that there didn't seem to be much lack of it when it came to erecting yet another honours board in the smoke room or lounge.

A three-course lunch in the Clubhouse went up to four shillings in 1951, but that was still cheaper than hiring a caddy, who wanted five.

Both religion and involvement in professional sport were questions to be answered on applications for membership at that time, so that Jews, Parsees or footballers might have found difficulty in penetrating the barriers of the more pretentious Scottish clubs. Or English ones, come to that.

In pursuit of revenue, a 'one-armed bandit' was installed in the smoke-room despite the Captain's objections, to be continually shifted to and from the lounge in efforts to placate his various supporters and opponents.

In the belief that the old Clubhouse had outlived its time, the Committee sought estimates for a new one. It was going to cost around £100,000. To raise the money it was planned to sell off the first and eighteenth fairways for housing development. The County Planning Officer told the Club that any attempt to do this would be resisted strongly at County Hall level.

In 1977 a new professional was appointed with a retainer of £1500 a year and was replaced when he left within the year with another at £2250. By 1980 the subs had topped £100 (guineas were no longer quoted) plus VAT.

In 1987 the big discussion was still how to replace the 82-year-old Clubhouse in time for the centenary celebrations. All the wiseacres were complaining about its obsolescence and general inadequacy compared to some of the imposing structures in the more up-market Clubs around. But the lovely old building had the last laugh on its detractors when the authorities designated it as a listed building of artistic merit to remain untouched on its present site. Which is how I left it.

And to summarise the history of Ranfurly Castle Golf Club the wording on the back label of the 1989 special Centenary Whisky Bottle commissioned to mark the occasion is featured on the following page.

Thank you, Robert Crampsey and the Ranfurly Castle Golf Club Limited for a fascinating story.

The Spirit of the Club

1889 - No bar facilities - centre of social activity was the Hotel.
1892 - Club House rented for £15 per annum.
1896 - Brandy 6/- per bottle, Whisky 24/- per gallon, Gin 3/6d
per bottle.
1910 - August - First Club Dinner - 6/- per ticket.
1910 - W. A. Cargill presented the clock to the Club.
1912 - December - Kilmacolm Club House destroyed by fire
given hospitality of our Club House and Course.
1915 - Balls were marked by machine to prevent them being
sold if found.
1917 - Members restricted to one glass per week and price
increased from 1/3d to 1/4d.
1932 - Ice introduced - cost 1d per drink.
1932 - April - Kilmacolm Annual Match cancelled due to
financial depression.
1932 - December - Club held Dinner to dispel general gloom
of international situation and hard Winter.
1936 - Purchase of new Whisky measure one third larger than
previous - known as Ranfurly Measure.
1939 - September - Whisky large 1/8d - Ranfurly measure
1/2d - Small 10d.
1942 - April - Only one case of Gin obtained in 4 months.
1945 - January - Whisky restricted to one glass per member
week days and two glasses per member Saturday and
Sunday.
1989 - All restrictions removed.

Reproduction of the back label specially produced for the Centenary
Whisky

15

Turnberry

O nce back in Troon, the car was turned over to the workshop mechanics while Colin and I went over mutual interests in his office. Within the hour the work was done, gratitude expressed, payment made, and farewells completed as yet another stage in an action-packed week drew to its close.

It was a little over eleven hours since I climbed from that hot tub at Gleneagles, during which time I'd motored 250 miles, visited Royal Troon Golf Club, Marine Highland Hotel, Colin Baird's offices, Ranfurly Castle Golf Club, had a new choke fitted, and sold 50 books. By this time more than a little weariness had crept into the Morley machine, and it was good to know that within another half-hour the rest of the day would be all downhill at Bill and Isa Milligan's at Maybole.

In 1954 I bought our Cuffley bungalow from the Milligans when they wanted to move into a larger house about 100 yards away. Twenty-one years after that Bill retired as director of an international engineering company and, as was always the plan, he and Isa returned to their native Ayrshire to live out their days just a few miles from where they started them. But instead of a 'wee-butt-and-ben' of yore they had a new bungalow built to their own design, with superb uninterrupted views across the Carrick Hills from its panoramic windows.

The Morleys had often been asked to come up and stay, but so far hadn't made it. But when putting together my sequence of visits and stopovers – and told by Marine Highland Hotel they had no room at the 'Inn' – I asked Bill over the phone if their offer still held good. It did. And my room with private bath, etc., was all ready on arrival without need for check-in formalities, form-filling, key-collection, or credit-card scrutiny and authorisation check. Nevertheless it was an unusual departure from established practice, as when away from home I book into hotels and refuse kindly offers of hospitality from friends and family alike – irrespective of house-size or the hospitable nature of the host.

A hotel room offers the same privacy as the four walls of your own home (unless you happen to live in a kibbutz or a V&W destroyer) and there's a lot to be said for being alone with your thoughts, or a good book in the bathroom, when the fancy takes you. And a hotel room can be left in cheerful disarray without a qualm – subject of course to a coin or two being left on the dressing table as 'qualm-balm' for the chambermaid – which is more than can be done at Auntie Nellie's. Or at the Milligans, come to that.)

The only decision I was asked to make was which of his four brands of malt or three of grain Bill was to slurp into a tumbler for me, to await my return after stowing possessions in bedroom and getting cleaned up.

We'd often played golf together when he lived close by, and it was a proud day for him, not too long after he went to live in Maybole, when he achieved membership of Turnberry Golf Club. He learned later – as did Peter Smiley, a good friend from Crews Hill Golf Club who achieved similar membership several years earlier on returning to his home in Ayrshire – that the euphoria can sour after a while.

Peter found the single-storey Clubhouse adjoining the golf shop not quite as palatial as the Hotel name would imply, and told of the 'grace-and-favour' status he and his fellow-members shared. Especially as far as playing the Ailsa – the Championship course closest to the sea – was concerned. Golf was the chief attraction for wealthy visitors who had travelled from afar just for the thrill of tackling the course they'd so often watched top golfers and celebrities playing on TV. And quite often a party of tourists or a business conference from Milwaukee, Osaka, Frankfurt, or wherever, would arrive to stay at the Hotel – looking to play on the Ailsa when the local members might have already had a match or competition planned.

Although Hotel bookings and golfing facilities would have been arranged well ahead, Peter complained there were many times when they weren't, due to an unexpected plane-load or coach-load of 'eager-beavers' arriving at times – or days – other than those scheduled. In such cases the Club members would be told they'd have to switch to the less scenic Arran course – and quite often at starting times other than those they'd originally planned to play on the Ailsa – as peak demand from the Hotel could well mean both courses being monopolised by hotel guests for a while.

Back in 1983 Reg Davies and I (yes, same old Reg Davies) had driven up to Turnberry to play a few rounds with Bill Milligan over a four-day stay, and booked ourselves into the Hotel. (When making our plans Bill tried his best to have us stay with them, but we insisted on the hotel as usual.)

Our friendly travel agent had been asked to book a couple of not-too-expensive rooms with all facilities – but not singles, as all too often, singles, in even the most prestigious hotels, are tucked away on top of the building with uninterrupted views of dustbins and boiler house in the courtyard below from tiny dormer windows. (Not, I hasten to add, that I know whether this applies at Turnberry.) Back he came with great glee to say he'd reserved a suite, consisting of two twin-bedded rooms, linked by a sitting room or lounge, at a special cheap rate because we'd picked a comparatively quiet time – I think it was early May.

But we couldn't believe our luck when, on checking in, we were taken up to a luxurious suite of rooms behind that magnificent façade, with our central windows under one of the second floor gabled ends. The one you always find yourself wondering enviously what it must be like staying there, when the TV camera features it – overlooking as it does everything panoramic Turnberry had to offer. On the mahogany sideboard in our sitting room was an array of bottles, glasses, fresh fruit, and dishes of 'nibbles'; while on the battered old upright piano with well-yellowed keys stood a bottle of Mumm Cordon Rouge in an ice-bucket, and the largest basket of fresh flowers with a card from the Hotel Manager saying, 'Welcome Mr and Mrs Morley!' So I got 'Mrs Morley' to open the champers and we toasted the Hotel Manager, our friendly travel agent, and the real Mrs Morley!

But the difference between the standing of a Turnberry Golf Club member and that of a guest at the Turnberry Hotel was clarified when I rang Bill to make plans for our golf on the next day. He suggested that all tee reservations and billing for same be done from our end as folks staying at the Hotel had preference for times, and paid less in green fees, than would a Club member when introducing his own guests. And this in fact proved to be the case.

On the occasion of this visit in 1989, though, Bill had long since left Turnberry Golf Club and, as a senior citizen, was getting his golf at a choice of eight well-manicured public courses in the area for an annual subscription of £55; and as

Turnberry Hotel from the Ailsa. *(From a 1910 picture postcard)*

The same famous façade – a bit wider and with a third gable-bay. *(From a 1990 brochure)*

he played about four times a week he reckoned it cost him about 19p a round! It went up in 1990 (what didn't?) but there's still a restricted membership scheme for the old folk which keeps them off the eight courses at specified peak times and still costs only £60 or so annually. I think they charge about twice that for one midweek round today at Wentworth!

Isa Milligan is a superb cook. We spent a couple of hours over her cordon bleu presentation of dinner that evening, during which we talked books, the places I'd so far been to in Scotland, mutual friends back home, and their daughter – Suzanne – son-in-law, grandchildren, and great-grandchild in Australia. Sheaves of photographs were produced relating to their golden wedding celebrations at their daughter's home in Woollagong, 40 miles from Sydney. She had secretly rustled up a piper, in full kilted regalia, to appear on the scene in conjunction with the serving of the special Anniversary Cake – a joint production by daughter and grand-daughter.

After they had ploughed through the various courses as set out on an elaborate menu – specially printed for the occasion and now framed and hung on the wall of the Milligan dining room – the assembled family clapped and cheered when the cake was brought in with due ceremony, and the camera caught Bill and Isa spellbound with surprise and emotion when, at the same time, the solitary piper rounded the corner of the house to the full drone of 'Scotland-the-Brave' wailing across the 'Bush'!

Over breakfast next morning we planned our day. I had an appointment with Christopher Rouse, general manager of Turnberry Hotel, at 10.30. Then it was back to Maybole for lunch, after which Bill and I were to play some golf at one of his eight courses. There was some difference of opinion when I refused to go along with their plans to dine at home that evening, putting up a good case instead for them to be my guests at a suitable hostelry of their choice. It horrified Isa that a guest in her house should pay today's exorbitant prices for food she considered to be far inferior to what she so enjoyed preparing herself. Nevertheless – after a short sharp verbal battle – I won the day and it was left to Bill to do the necessary research and booking while I was at Turnberry.

A friendly receptionist found me a king-size marketing pack to browse through while Christopher Rouse was tied up with an earlier appointment. It was just as well she did as, by the time he was through, I'd read the lot and learned enough of Turnberry's history for its presentation here.

The Marquis of Ailsa, Captain of Prestwick Golf Club in 1899, was hooked on the game and felt the need to get his handicap down with some practice a little nearer home. So in 1901 he had his own golf course built in the grounds of Culzean Castle – pronounced 'Cullene' and about 4 miles from Turnberry. The layout was entrusted to Willie Fernie, winner of the Open in 1883, and runner-up in 1882, 1884, and 1890. His son, Tom, was Turnberry's first professional.

The Marquis probably felt he'd gone a bit over the top with a golf course to keep and maintain just for himself and a few friends to knock around on, because in 1901 he sold it to the Glasgow and South Western Railway. Aware of its potential as a 'little earner', the new owners wasted little time in building a hotel, a station, a branch line from Ayr, and a schedule of frequent local trains – plus direct sleeper services from London and the Midlands.

The $19\frac{1}{2}$ mile single track line, passing through the heart of Burns-country, was reckoned to provide its passengers with one of the most scenic journeys in the land. It needed a total of 65 bridges, 2 viaducts and 6 culverts to negotiate the craggy, undulating coastal area. The new railway line was opened to the public – as was the new, 100-bedroom Turnberry Hotel – on 17 May 1906.

The Hotel was publicised (remember, this was 20 years before Gleneagles) as being a haven for golfers, with 'ultra-modern' electric light, controlled heating and ventilation throughout, lifts to all floors, and 'suites of special bathrooms incorporating plunge baths, showers and simulated waves with hot, cold, and salt water'.

On Saturdays, express trains left Glasgow at 1pm with a dining car for golfers, and one with a 'tea-car' took them back at 5.

Sunday golf was introduced at Turnberry in 1909, and its first ever major golfing event was the Ladies British Open Amateur Championship in 1912.

But hardly had the place really started to capture the imagination than along came 1914 and World War One. The course was requisitioned as a training establishment for the Royal Flying Corps, and the Hotel as an officer's mess for Canadians.

It was another five years before the Government gave the place back to the railway company, who then wasted little time in restoring it to its former glory and building a second 18-hole golf course. By 1926 the London Midland and Scottish Railway had taken over the Glasgow and South Western – as they did Gleneagles and the Caledonian Railway – and named the two Turnberry courses as the Ailsa and the Arran. The Ailsa is the one seen so often on television, with unique scenic features, like a sparkling ocean with the Isle of Arran in the distance; the spectacular 9th with adjacent lighthouse; the blue-grey rocky island of Ailsa Craig; and the multi-gabled façade of the Hotel – all combining to provide one of the most picturesque golfing venues in the world. Weather permitting! And weather at Turnberry can range from awful to diabolical on a bad day – or week!

As motor cars and bus services came into their own, so the railway found there weren't so many people needing trains for getting to and from Turnberry. The writing was on the wall, and the last passenger train to run in or out of Turnberry Station was in November 1930. But by this time the Hotel and golf courses were renowned and their future assured.

Came World War Two and Turnberry was again conscripted to serve its country. This time with RAF Coastal Command. The courses were levelled out with earth-moving machinery and acres of concrete laid, so that mighty warplanes laden with bombs and depth-charges could tackle the U-boat menace to Allied shipping on the Western Approaches. The Hotel became a hospital.

When the war ended nobody thought that vast concrete acreage could ever be reconverted to golf courses. In 1946 the Directors of the Railway voted to write it off as a golfing centre. That is, all except their Chairman, Frank Hole. He said, 'Machines turned our fairways into runways – well, if we can get the Government to put up enough cash in compensation we can get machines to change them back to fairways.'

With convincing rhetoric he fought and won the day. Soon, powerful bulldozers were chopping up the concrete and fleets of trucks carting the debris to the nearby coastal village of Maidens, where it was used to build a sea wall. Mackenzie Ross, top Scottish architect, made models in Plasticine of the fairway shapes and contours he wanted, and with James Alexander, Superintendent of British Transport Hotels, in charge of the work, Turnberry's magnificent courses were painstakingly re-created and improved to standards of even greater glory than pre-war. Thirty thousand cubic yards of topsoil were dug from surrounding fields, mixed with peat, and laid in accordance with specialist instructions. The Ailsa made history in being the first British golf course to be turfed throughout instead of seeded, and was reopened in 1951. The Arran was ready for play in 1954. It wasn't long before top events were again being played at Turnberry, and in 1961 Michael Bonallack won his first British Championship title there.

In 1963 the Ailsa hosted the Walker Cup, and in 1977 its first Open: a show-stopper that nobody who watched it will ever forget. With Nicklaus trailing Watson by one shot at the final hole and the rest of the field nowhere, he put a prodigious drive among bushes in a shallow gully out on the right. Watson made no mistake in hitting two 'fairway-splitters', leaving a putt of a couple of feet for a birdie and the Championship. But the unflappable Nicklaus then crashed an iron shot from his unfriendly lie on to the edge of the green, and sank a 30-or-40-foot putt for his unbelievable birdie. But the equally unflappable Watson didn't miss his either, and Turnberry's first Open was over.

It was Greg Norman who won Turnberry's next Open in 1986, which again must have set a few records in being played over four days of the most atrocious weather the Competition had seen in its 126 years.

When the Government decided to sell off its chain of Transport Hotels, the Turnberry complex was bought by John Sherwood, the American entrepreneur who runs Sea Containers, Orient Express, a world-wide string of luxury hotels, and many other enterprises. A lot of money was poured in over the next nine years to bring the Hotel up to maximum splendour, but in 1987 Turnberry was considered too expensive to run for what was really a seasonal business and sold to a Japanese consortium. Since when millions have again been poured into restoring its palatial glories, in order to encourage the big-spending fraternity to flock in from all parts of the globe.

The marketing pack included a leaflet describing how Turnberry's lighthouse, often described as its 'trademark', stands on the site of Turnberry Castle. In 1306, King Robert the Bruce, one of Ayrshire's favourite sons, – the other of course being Robert Burns – secretly returned to Scotland from exile after his celebrated encounter with a spider, and with a small force surprised and overpowered the English garrison of Turnberry Castle. For the next eight years he went around the country being a general nuisance to the English armies of Edward I and, when he died, Edward II – who were just as much of a nuisance to the Scots; until Robert decided in 1314 to go to the aid of his countrymen beleaguered in Stirling Castle, where a large force of English had been laying siege for some time.

The 'big match' was held at a little village called Bannockburn, about 6 miles from Stirling, and Scotland won 10,000 to 4,000. (That's how many of the opposition's supporters they were each said to have despatched.)

As a result of Bruce and his merry men inflicting further indignities on the invading forces, Scotland won its independence at the Declaration of Arbroath in 1320. But having got the taste for 'home internationals' they carried on making themselves unpopular in the north of England until the Treaty of Northampton in 1328, when everybody eventually agreed to stop squabbling. Never has Scotland owed so much to one man, born and bred in the Carrick Hills, just a few miles from Turnberry, who died of leprosy in 1329 at the age of 55. (And most of this learned from a hotel booklet while waiting to talk to its manager about my own books.)

Christopher Rouse, yet another Englishman in charge of a multi-million pound Scottish leisure development, said he'd been managing at Turnberry for the past 12½ years, and many of his key staff had worked there for more than double that time. Having served three different owners he felt the Hotel was now entering the greatest period in its history, and was proud of the confidence shown him by his Japanese employers. They left him to run things as he saw fit while continuing to provide finance as necessary for whatever was needed to further enhance the Turnberry image. Like similar leisure establishments described earlier in the book, they were anxious to encourage non-golfers to visit and indulge themselves in the extensive forms of activity and hedonism the place was geared to provide.

With regard to my books, he explained there were no shops as such in the Hotel, but the Hall Porter sold from a stock provided and replenished by book wholesalers in Prestwick. I was taken to meet Bob Jamieson, Turnberry Golf Shop manager and pro for many years. He'd read the book I'd sent to Christopher Rouse and knew some of the characters featured in my stories. He stocked up with six copies and, once again, an American in the shop at the time noticing the delivery of books immediately bought a copy and had me sign it.

Back at the Hotel, Alan Hall the Hall Porter, or Concierge as it says on the card he gave me, asked if I'd supply him through his wholesaler and gave their phone number. A bookshop opened in the Hotel about a year later, much to the relief of Mr Hall. It put an end to his constant need to remind visitors that the copies on display by his desk in the foyer were for browsing and buying – not a free, self-service library facility!

Before closing the chapter, I'd like to add that there's hardly a week goes by without reading of yet another multi-million pound-or-dollar venture to be built around golf in Britain or elsewhere. Modest plans for a common-or-garden private Club just for playing golf are now considered to be uneconomical and 'old hat'. Everybody is busy pouring money (usually somebody else's) into ambitious schemes with championship-length golf courses, heated pools, squash courts, gymnasiums, a gourmet selection of restaurants and bars, and sumptuous accommodation.

Yet I suppose Turnberry was the very first in that league. It's now almost 90 years since the Glasgow and West of Scotland Railway incorporated first-class golf as part of the fun, when planning a luxury retreat for confirmed pleasure-seekers amid the wild and woolly coastal regions of Scotland. And as a practising hedonist myself, I'd say Turnberry is still in a class of its own in that respect.

————16————

Prestwick

Once back with the Milligans, I phoned Carrick Books in Prestwick to tell them the concierge at Turnberry Hotel thought he could sell my book, and would they arrange to send him half-a-dozen. With the Open to be held at Troon in a couple of months they liked the sound of a new golf book and asked to see a sample copy. 'Yes, it'll be with you in about an hour', they were told, as Bill said we could call into Prestwick after lunch before going on to golf at Belleisle.

The place took some finding in among factory and airline-service buildings around Prestwick Airport, but when we did it was a busy and well-stocked warehouse, where the manager examined my sample with a colleague before ordering 40 copies. Very gratifying.

But having got as far as the town of Prestwick it would have been sacrilege to leave without taking a look at its famous Golf Club – although once again, it was not one of those on the original schedule.

Let St Andrews, Musselburgh, The Hon. Golfers, The Burgess, Bruntsfield, or Royal Blackheath lay their conflicting claims to being the birthplace of competitive golf, there's no parallel dispute over the birthplace of the Open Championship – the World's oldest and greatest international golfing event. Yet it all started as an idea in a five-year-old Club back in 1856 – a Club probably unknown to most of the above-named veterans planning their hundredth birthday-parties around that time – give or take a few years.

Prestwick was a Burgh of about 1000 acres on the west coast of Scotland, 2½ miles north of Ayr, in the year 1600. That was the date when under the Royal Charter of King James each of its 36 Freemen (Prestwick's total adult male population at the time) was presented with a 999-year lease to 14 to 16 acres of it. Two hundred years later there were 66 dwelling houses and 266 persons in the Burgh, of whom one-fifth were under seven years of age. They were described as being in a very poor state, 'many of them Fishers, Colliers, and Salters'.

In 1851 a number of the gentry residing in the surrounding area, who were prone to meet and knock a ball about on Prestwick Links (a lozenge of common land bound by the ocean on the one side and the Glasgow and South Western Railway on the other) thought they would emulate their 'eastern brethren' and form themselves into a Golf Club. (I do believe that they, too, may have been practising Freemasons at the time.)

Once again, these weren't from the lower or middle-class orders as, when the initial circulars were sent to 69 of them, among the 57 who said 'count me in!' were such names as Lord Eglinton, Lord Charles Kerr, Lord Colville, Sir James Boswell, Sir H H Campbell, Sir Thomas Moncrieff, Sir David Baird, Sir James Ferguson, and General Sir Hope Grant. There were others with no titles mentioned but it's a safe bet none was a fisher, collier or salter – nor were they drawn from the local butchery-, bakery-, or candlestick-makery-classes!

The first meeting was held at the Red Lion Hotel in July 1851, and in his absence Lord Eglinton was elected the first Captain of Prestwick Golf Club. Tom Morris became Keeper of the Green at 15s. per week, and the Links on which they laid out their 12-hole course was rented from 12 Freemen for the total sum of £6 a year.

There was no Clubhouse, and players changed and kept their clubs in a rented room near the Red Lion – whose landlord would come out with a basket on each arm laden with food and drink, to provide lunch during a match or competition. It was taken alfresco or in the 'lunch hut' – site of the current greenkeeping sheds – depending on weather.

In October 1856, just five years after that inaugural meeting of this far-western outpost of 'Clubland', but still with just a rented room and a hut in which to eat their 'take-away pub-lunch', Prestwick was anxious to mingle with the 'big-brothers' back East. They hit on the idea of starting a Golf Tournament for Scotland, to which each Scottish Club – and Blackheath – was invited to enter a maximum of two players; and wrote to the Royal and Ancient suggesting it be played at St Andrews in July 1857. Reading between the lines again in search of the real story, I'd say the underlying intention was to create an opportunity for the boys from 'Indian country' to visit and mix as equals with the Eastern hierarchy in the R&A's palatial new Clubhouse.

The history books tell us the tournament never took place, but nobody really tries to explain why. Well, in my opinion there's no mystery. As far as the R&A was concerned, it was just like our village tennis club inviting the Queen to their annual dinner dance and can they please hold it at Windsor Castle! Bear in mind the more chauvinistic element of East Scottish society considered the Western half of their country to be peopled by semi-barbarians – much the same as some of our 'City-slickers' in the South feel about over-involvement with anywhere north of Watford!

Ah! Here he comes with mine, at last!

So Prestwick Golf Club decided to go it alone, and maybe in the fullness of time the mountain would come to Mahomet. And it did!

According to James E. Shaw, author of *Prestwick Golf Club*, published by Jackson, Son & Company of Glasgow in 1938, there were eight competitors at Prestwick for that first Competition on 17 October 1860. The winner was to receive a Championship Belt, to be

> left with the Treasurer of the Club until he produce a guarantee to the satisfaction of the above Committee that the Belt shall be safely kept and laid on the table at the next Meeting to compete for it until it become the property of the winner by being won three years in succession and that under a penalty of £25 sterling.

Played over three rounds of 12 holes each, in the one day, it was won by Willie Park of Musselburgh with 174 strokes.

Ten professionals – three from Musselburgh, two from Prestwick, two from Blackheath, and one each from St Andrews, Bruntsfield and Perth – plus eight amateurs of which only two finished, competed in 1861, when the winner was Old Tom Morris with 163 strokes.

The momentous decision was made on the eve of that meeting that henceforth the Competition would be open for all the world, both professional and amateur, to compete. Nevertheless only eight again took part in 1862 with Tom Morris completing the 36 holes in 163 strokes. Willie Park was second, trailing by 13 shots!

The next year they put up prize money to encourage more entries and attracted 14 to take part. The winner still had to be content with just the honour of the Championship Belt, but 2nd, 3rd and 4th received £5, £3, and £2 respectively.

On 16 September 1864 the winner received £6 to go with the Belt. Entries were down to 12 professionals, but 4 amateurs put the field up to 16.

The numbers stayed low right through to 1870, when 17 competed and Young Tom Morris, now 19 years old, won the Belt for the third consecutive time, with an all-time record score of 149! That's five-over-fours for 36 holes with hickory shafts and 'guttie' balls!

In accordance with the Rules, the Championship Belt then became young Tom's property, and with nothing to play for no Competition was held in 1871. It's always puzzled me why, with an unbroken record of 11 consecutive annual prestigious events under its own belt, and a year to think about it after the original prize had been won, Prestwick didn't try to maintain some form of continuity with an alternative trophy. But judging by problems in getting members to pay minimal dues – as told later – big-spending on baubles for others to win wasn't everybody's idea of a good time, and appeals to finance further Open Competitions for image-enhancement purposes were rejected by the tight-fisted element in the Club.

The chapter on Muirfield describes how the Open Championship re-started at Prestwick in 1872 with a Claret Cup as the trophy. And one of those on St Andrews explains how the original Claret Cup sits permanently in a glass case at the R&A, while a replica is made every year for the winner to take away and keep. The trophy was bought jointly by Prestwick, St Andrews, and the Hon. Golfers of Edinburgh, each of which hosted the Open annually in rotation in that order from 1872. So the event did in fact finally reach 'Windsor Castle' in 1873!

The cash prize to the winner stayed at £6, until it went up to £10 at St Andrews in 1876. That really was a 'red-letter' year, according to an article in the June 1990 issue of *Round the Green*, the quarterly magazine of the British Golf Collectors' Society. It was by Robert Burnet, historian to the R&A, and taken from his book, *The St Andrews Opens*, published by John Donald of Edinburgh.

In those days the Open was held at the end of the playing season. Illustrious members of those Clubs had spent August on the grouse moors, and needed September to sharpen up their game and play off competitions, before congregating to watch and wager on the Open in the rapidly shortening days of a Scottish October. To get 36 holes in, the first competitors had to start at 9am and finish lunch in time to tee off for the second 18 at 12.15pm. (By which time today, some of our 'high-speed' performers would just about have reached the turn in the morning round!)

Prince Leopold of the Belgians had not long been made Captain of the R&A and, in the general excitement, the Club had forgotten to book the course for the Open to be played on the following Saturday! (Well, it was only the second time there and three years had passed since they first had it!) With the result that the 34 entries had to alternate with those Club members, artisans, and would-be golfers among the general public at large who had already booked starting times.

In the gathering gloom and anxiety to finish, players were hitting out for distant greens before those in front had putted out. David Strath, having already knocked out an artisan with a wayward shot on the 14th, was again in trouble when his shot to the 17th was stopped from finishing on the notorious Road through striking another competitor on the leg. He finished the 36 holes to tie with Bob Martin for first place on 176. But when the competitor he struck called for his disqualification through being in breach of the relevant rule, Strath decided to withdraw from the play-off and accept second place!

Prestwick now hosted the Competition every three years but it was never as popular a venue as the other two were over those first 20 years. They each held seven Opens during that period, with Prestwick averaging 26 entries a year, St Andrews 48, and Musselburgh (with the 7th at Muirfield) 40. It was at Muirfield in 1892 that the Open switched to its present format of 72 holes.

The last Open Championship held at Prestwick was in 1925, when 200 entries competed for the £100 first prize; compared to Hoylake with 277 entries the previous year and Lytham St Annes with 293 in the following one. Prestwick conceived this delicate creature and nursed it through a difficult childhood, but the Open had now grown to be a lusty youth and there was no longer room for it round the old family hearth. Prestwick's physical limitations, such as inadequate facilities for spectators and parking, lack of space for the by now essential tented-city, and crowd control problems during play, meant that Prestwick had to retire from the coveted rota of Belt-cum-Championship venues 65 years ago, with a record 24 'hostings' to its credit – a total that only St Andrews will be able to match in July 1990. Yet the R&A would have been comfortably in the lead if they hadn't been so 'Windsor Castle-ish' in 1856! But with its prominent spot in Golf's Hall of Fame assured for all time, let us unfold a little more of Prestwick Golf Club's history other than the big event it started.

Despite its ambitious aims, Prestwick Golf Club was quite happy to go on changing clothes in a rented room and taking lunch from a publican's basket for the first 15 years of its existence. But in 1867, what with now having hosted seven Championships and seen its membership nearing the 100 mark, ambition demanded something a bit more up-market as far as amenities were concerned. Many of the

Clubs written about hitherto built modestly at first and went in for something bigger and better as time rolled by. But not Prestwick. The impressive two-storey Clubhouse built in 1868 at a cost of £758 still stands today (with extensions and improvements added over the years); living proof that overriding gloom-laden forecasts of bankruptcy by opposition members was well justified at the time.

It wasn't an easy Club to run in the early days, with its members drawn from outlying parts of the country and needing a train or couple of hours on a horse or in a horse-drawn cart to reach the coast for a game. Many of the 60 members in 1853 thought the £1 annual subscription a bit over the top and let their membership lapse. But others took their place and there were 78 on the books the following year – but with quite a number still in arrears.

In 1858 there was a £17 deficiency in the annual profit and loss accounts and after members at the AGM voted in favour of adopting the Treasurer's motion that no further requests for expenditure be made, came an immediate vote in favour of spending £10 on silver medals. 'Twas ever thus with Committees – whether formed to deal with leisure pursuits, communal activities, or national interests; they all enjoy squandering hard-to-acquire funds on frivolous 'toys' and non-essentials.

Year after year the minutes showed troubles with recurring arrears and inherent weaknesses in decision-making were self-evident. In 1862, a 'draconian' ruling that anyone more than one year in arrears with his subscription could not play, had to be watered down to two years in order to placate objectors to the harshness of the edict! It was still only £1 a year at that time. A motion was carried in 1869 that an annual fee of 5s. green-money be paid by anybody using the Links, whether member or not. But very few paid.

Subscriptions were raised to £2 in 1885 and the entrance fee to £15 in 1888. By 1892 there were 418 members and a healthy credit balance of £815 7s. 3d. in the accounts, but getting the actual money in was just as difficult as ever. In 1897 subscriptions for existing members were raised to £2.10s. and £3 for new entries, the Committee threatening to resign en bloc if the motion was again turned down – as earlier attempts to improve the Club's solvency had been. They won the day this time. The money was badly needed to meet debentures, bonds and overdrafts incurred in developing the Club's interests.

In 1914 two members resigned when the subs went up by a further ten shillings, but there's no record of any further objections when they reached £5 in 1921.

Annual increases were avoided in 1928 when members were asked to take up a new issue of debentures, so that all bonds and mortgages could be paid off; the issue was over-subscribed. Obviously a new generation of membership had developed with a sense of financial awareness in place of those parsimonious pioneers who expected so much but resented paying for it. And that is how, in 1928, Prestwick Golf Club became the sole owner of all the land it occupied together with the building standing on it.

It is now 1990, and looking back over the years there is no shortage of landmarks. Particularly the centenary celebrated in 1951. That was marked by a special Stroke Competition, won by a member who had held a scratch handicap for the past four decades.

It was at Prestwick in 1890 that John Ball of Hoylake was the first of only three amateurs ever to win the Open having already won the first of his eight British Amateur Championships there in 1888.

The handsome 127-year-old Clubhouse is still an all-male

preserve, into which ladies are invited for a Club function once a year. There is no Ladies Club as such at Prestwick Golf Club, but the gentler sex have permission to play the course on a grace-and-favour basis. They also have the use of a second-floor room for food and changing purposes.

The course is reckoned to be 'a golf architect's dream of Heaven with all his materials in the form of sandhills, winding valleys, and tortuous rushing stream at his ready disposal', said Frank Pennink – English Amateur Champion in 1937 and 1938 – in his book *Golf*, published by Peter Garnett in 1952. Back in 1890, the *Saturday Review* published an article on Prestwick Golf Club, saying the course was the most picturesque in the country. To close the chapter, here's a golfer's attitude to scenic beauty as described above – plus a description of the opening holes at Prestwick – taken from that same magazine:

. . . But all the scenery, in the opinion of the golfer, [*says the writer who seems to have cracked the eternal philosophy of the game*] has nothing to do with it. It doesn't affect him and, except when he is very many holes up, or very many holes down so that a match has lost all its interest, and he has ceased to be a golfer and becomes only an ordinary human being, he does not even look at it.

But there is beauty in the undulations of the Prestwick Links that affect him not as a human being, but in his real self, as a golfer. The course is so hilly, so faced with bold bunker cliffs, all the hazards on so grand a scale, the sandhills so mountainous, and the burn so worthy of its name.

How many golfers have been so sadly disillusioned on first sight of that famous Swilken Burn of St Andrews of which so much has been heard? A burn! It has such a fine moorland sound. You can almost hear it rushing over its stones. And what does he find? A muddy little dribble worming along ignominiously at a crawl between little stone walls, as it would never get to the sea. An eel would scorn to live in it.

But the Prestwick burn is the real article. It bustles along at a good merry pace between green banks, and will carry your ball far away down before you can overtake it – if you ever do. A trout might live in it. It is said that many do and that their flesh is of a peculiar elastic firmness and piquant flavour, which analysis shows to be due to the presence of gutta percha in large quantities.

Prestwick itself is a nice little collection of villas. It has a beach and sands. It is but a few minutes run on the train from Ayr and from Prestwick Station to the Clubhouse goes a private passage sacred to members only. The vulgar hordes are kept at a discreet distance.

On the first hole, Prestwick golfers tee their balls in front of the Clubhouse with the railway to the right. A heeled ball can well finish up through the window of a passing train, in which case you telegraph for it to the Station Master at Troon.

The second hole can be reached in one but think yourself lucky if you do it in three.

A fine drive to the third brings you to the brink of a deep, deep bunker named, with fitting reverence, 'Cardinal's Nob'. On its right runs the burn, where dwell the trout that batten-and-fatten on golf balls. The Nob rises on the other side of the bunker, a great cliff of sand, shored up with timbers of black and forbidding aspect. It was in this famous bunker that a new system of counting was inaugurated. 'How many have you played?', asked a golfer who had patiently waited while his opponent bounced shot after against the black timbers. 'I don't know' said the sufferer, wearily. 'I went in at half past eleven and have been playing ever since. It's ten minutes to twelve now – you work it out!'

There ends a chapter on yet another famous Golf Club of which I've no playing experience, but with a unique and colourful history etched far deeper in to the Morley cerebral 'computer' than any sub-par golfing performance could ever have programmed had I played there.

Belleisle

Driving south out of Prestwick on busy roads – with skies even busier with traffic in and out of its international airport – we headed for Belleisle, about a mile south of Ayr.

Belleisle being one of the eight public courses on which Bill's senior citizen membership card gave him privileged playing rights, he had no difficulty earlier that day in booking us a starting time over the phone. But having spent longer in Prestwick than anticipated we were now a good half hour over the top, and our hope of a game lay in the possibility of being able to slot in somewhere. Possible it proved to be, after Bill's friendly word with the Starter. He told me afterwards that he'd explained his guest was an author up from London for the express purpose of writing a history of Belleisle – among other famous Scottish courses – but was already over-running his crowded programme due to time spent with Prestwick Golf Club.

Well, they didn't actually clear the course for us there and then, but we were allowed to strike off as soon as we were ready; the four-ball already assembled on the tee giving us a cheery greeting and the courtesy of the tee after the Starter had gone across to chat with them. Thankfully we both hit a reasonable drive: all too often an invitation to play through finishes up with the ball bolting into thick rough 25 yards away and 30 degrees off line.

Belleisle Golf Course takes its title from the mansion of that name, built in 1775 and reconstructed in 1829. In 1898 it was bought by Lord Glentanar, who sought permission from the French authorities to reproduce the two dining rooms as copies of the Music Room and Marie Antoinette's boudoir in the Palace of Versailles.

In 1926 he went to live in Aberdeenshire and sold Belleisle and its surrounding land to Ayr Corporation, with the understanding that the whole estate would be preserved in its natural beauty. The Corporation called in James Braid – yes, old James Braid again – to lay out two 18-hole golf courses. They were named Belleisle and Seafield. Both were opened on 10 September 1927 with a 36-hole match between James Braid and Alex Hurd on the one side, playing two well-known local amateurs.

The ground floor of the mansion was converted to a Clubhouse, and the upper floors became a natural history museum. But as the museum turned out to be a bit of a 'white elephant' it is now part of the three-star, 17-bedroom, Belleisle House Hotel.

Our game that afternoon was only two days after my ill-fated knock on the pitch-and-putt at Gleneagles, the nightmare memory of which still weighed heavily on me as we walked down that first fairway. But all went reasonably well until it became necessary to play a controlled half-shot – with inevitable results. Nevertheless it was a beautiful undulating course in perfect condition, and a delight to play on in the hot afternoon sunshine. Losing three balls was a cheap price to pay for the pleasure derived, especially as only one of them was due to a wayward shot. The other two

Belleisle Hotel façade

were won by Bill who, playing level, pipped me by one shot over twelve holes – all we really had time to play. And I promised if ever this story was written, his birdie-two on the 7th – the 'Wee Neat' – would get an honourable mention. [*How's that, Bill?*]

On putting our clubs back in the boot of my car, a stern-looking gentleman came towards us from where he'd been sitting in his own near by.

'I've been sitting over there for the best part of an hour, keeping a protective eye on yours', he said, making no effort to hide his annoyance. 'You locked up all your doors right enough, but not your electrically-operated windows. When I came out here to put my own clubs away and drive off, there were two youths with their heads stuck through the wide-open window of your driving door. I chased them off and have kept watch ever since – and I believe they've been doing the same, waiting in the distance for me to leave. We've had a lot of trouble here recently with thieves breaking into parked cars, without people like you coming along and making things doubly easy for the villains.'

Sheepishly explaining how authors are renowned for careless stupidity in their everyday affairs, I thanked him for his 'neighbourhood watchfulness' and pressed a signed copy of *If if wasn't for Golf . . . !* on him in appreciation. He's also down for one of *By Yon Bonnie Links*, too, if Bill sends me his address.

At the beginning of the Turnberry chapter I wrote of difficulty in getting the Milligans out to dinner. Victory became mine in the end by playing on Isa's enthusiasm for 'Rabbie' Burns – she could, and did, recite yards of his stuff from the top of her head – and by expressing a wish to know more of the bard and his links with the surrounding countryside. With the result that we were booked to eat at his old cowshed on Mount Oliphant Farm.

Well, that's what it was when Burns lived there with his parents in the 1770s. But now the old cowshed is a listed building, and was opened to the public in 1986 as the Burns Byre Restaurant.

According to the records, 'William Burnes', the bard's dad, paid £40 a year for the farm when he moved there in 1776. Two hundred and thirteen years later, a fine cordon bleu meal for three with aperitifs and a bottle of wine came out at a little over a year's rent. Very good value, we all agreed, and Bill said, 'If you write about it, Sam, remember to mention the cattle were let out before they started serving the food!'

At 9.30 the following morning we exchanged fond farewells – me to start on my way home; Bill on his way to play golf with a friend coming over from Glasgow; and Isa to get the sheets off my bed, into the washing machine, on to the line, and she reckoned on having them ironed and in the closet by the time I was crossing the Border into England.

In accordance with my original plans there was to be a final rendezvous with a Mr Carruthers, Secretary of Lockerbie Golf Club, the fourth of those on my list with a centenary in 1989. But his enthusiasm over the phone when planning my visit ten days earlier had apparently waned by the time I got there on Saturday morning. All I could find was a young greenkeeper who said, 'Mr Carruthers was awa' to Peebles the day', but had told him that I might be calling with a message. Did I have one to give him? After belting the bejasus out of my engine for the past two and a half hours to get there for the appointed time – although about half an hour late, I must admit – there was only one message to give. But there was no point in venting spleen on that nice young man. Especially as he seemed to have his hands full taking green fees from four stroppy Englishmen in the toolshed, and offering one of them who asked to hire a trolley the use of his own as the Club didn't have any to hire.

Poor old Lockerbie! I still have vivid memories of the fresh wreaths lining the road up to the church after its horrible Pan Am disaster just five months before my visit.

There were no plans for a book at the time of that call, let alone the title now chosen for it. Had that meeting with Mr Carruthers taken place and a chapter on Lockerbie Golf Club included here, then my 'Mixed Bag of Auld Clubs' would have numbered 15, not 14. Anyone with even an elementary knowledge of the Rules of Golf knows that having more than 14 clubs in a golf bag incurs a penalty. Perhaps in this instance the book itself might have been disqualified. So thank you Mr Carruthers!

Being Saturday afternoon, motorway traffic on the run south was comfortably light, with the result that – after a stop for lunch near Preston – I was coasting down the home stretch at Cuffley a little after 5pm. But not before a long overdue session at our local car-wash. Having covered some 1200 miles since leaving the house five-and-a-half days earlier, there were at least three layers of road dust covering every square inch of visible metalwork – not to mention a windscreen that could have been a mine of information to any student of insect after-life.

I had tried to get some of it off back in Scotland, but found automatic car-washes a bit thin on the ground north of the Tweed. 'Up here we wash oor ain!', was the dour reply when enquiring for the nearest Auto-wash during my travels. But being a self-indulgent septuagenarian from the South, I preferred to sit nice and dry listening to a soothing cassette midst a mass of whirling brushes, rather than go back to the old bucket, sponge, and hosepipe routine involved in 'washin' ma ain'!

Epilogues were often used to sum up and provide a moral to the stories of yesterday. As *By Yon Bonnie Links* delves into the good old days throughout its 17 chapters a brief one shouldn't be out of place here:

EPILOGUE

Whether from The Highlands, Lowlands, Netherlands, Midlands – or Papua New Guinea – addicts the world over acknowledge Scotland as the 'Holy Land' of GOLF. This light-hearted story of a pilgrimage across that 'Holy Land' among those who worship at its shrine, should leave little doubt that Golf and its history needn't be quite as awesome as some would have us believe.

Acknowledgements

Oone of the great pleasures in writing *By Yon Bonnie Links!* was delving into the vast amount already written on the history of Golf, and the enthusiastic help received from those who knew so much more of the subject than its author did to begin with.

Whenever possible I have tried to name my sources of information and express appreciation to those who kindly permitted me to quote from or paraphrase their work. To any who may feel that I should have sought permission but didn't, please accept my apologies.

But whether they be named or not, I am equally grateful to all whose written or oral contributions are included in my story.

Among those deserving a special vote of thanks, and in order of appearance in the text, are the following:

Mark Wilson for his flattering Foreword.

Michael Bonallack for inspiring the idea of an 'expedition' and being so helpful with detail on St Andrews and the R&A.

Bill Robertson for initiating the idea of writing this 'Chronicle'.

Patric Dickinson for his whimsical style in *A Round of Golf Courses*.

David White for the unstinting provision of books and memorabilia that opened my eyes to the fascinating history of Scotland as the birthplace of Golf and its links with Freemasonry.

David Stirk whose publications, knowledge, letters and encouraging advice have helped so much in producing my own story.

David Hamilton for his invaluable help on the Musselburgh chapter.

Adam Latto – likewise, especially for his artistic impression of 'Mrs Forman's' inn as it stands today.

Ian Hume for so much of 'The Burgess' story.

Archie Walker for the Weiskopf 'gem' related on page 84!

Jim Horsfield for the 'essential ingredients' to the Auchterlonie story.

Alma Robertson ditto for the LGU story.

Sir Richard Bonallack who called in his cousin, *Basil,* to help in preparing the family's 'smuggling history' for me.

Ian Wilson and the Souvenir Book for so much information on Gleneagles.

Laurence Viney for his encyclopaedic knowledge of golfing history, and availability at all times to provide data and correct my ramblings when necessary.

Bill and Isa Milligan for the warmth of their hospitality and assistance with research.

The Unknown Gentleman who guarded my car in the Belleisle Car Park (p214)!

Susan Floyd, my daughter, for the jacket design.

Helen Wightwick, who hardly ever complained about re-typing my re-hashed typescripts over the past 14 months!

Finally, here's yet another Morley tome highlighted with *Jo Varney* drawings – each of them originating from a couple of lines of text. Thank you, Jo, you're unique!

16th August, 1990

Index